TRAIN JOURNEYS
IN
VIKING LANDS

by *TERRY PLANT*

First published in Great Britain in 1974 by
Terry Plant, 11 Lyndhurst Avenue, Kingskerswell,
Newton Abbot, Devon

Second Edition 1978
Third Edition 1984
Fourth Edition 1986
Fifth Edition 1989

ISBN 0 9510511 0 5

Also by Terry Plant
VIKING JOURNEY TO HAPPINESS

For Children
LEIF THE REINDEER
HENRY THE GOAT
THE HAPPY LITTLE TRAIN

Printed and bound by Short Run Press Ltd, Bittern Road,
Sowton Industrial Estate, Exeter.

This book gives many vivid impressions of the writer's travel throughout the Scandinavian lands. Having lived and worked in Norway, Sweden, and Denmark, he has been fortunate to have made many contacts and made strong friendships with the hardy peoples of these fascinating lands. This had given a greater understanding towards their customs and working lives.

Included too are many highly interesting facts concerning the development of the State Railways, with Norway and Sweden in particular. Having travelled from the West Coast of Norway to the Russian frontier of East Finland, and from the busy streets of Copenhagen to the wilds of Swedish Lapland, much can be related.

It gives great pleasure to express experiences of travel and friendly contacts with people of all occupations so that others may benefit.

Sincere gratitude is given to the Norwegian, Finnish, Icelandic, Swedish, and Danish Embassies in London who have given spontaneous help and useful information. The Norwegian, Swedish, and Finnish State Railways have given the opportunity of seeing the splendid natural beauty of the Northern lands, and visiting beautiful capitals and hospitable towns and villages nestling in peaceful green valleys.

The strong ties of friendship with the energetic, enterprising Scandinavian peoples has given the inspiration and interest to make this journey possible.

TERRY PLANT

TRAIN JOURNEYS IN VIKING LANDS

by Terry Plant

For many years the writer has travelled thousands of miles throughout the Scandinavian lands by trains and public transport, from Bergen in the South, to Bodo and Narvik in the North. The trains make travel a great pleasure, and even above the Arctic Circle, in Norway, Finland, and Sweden, they form an important link for trade and those more fortunate individuals who have fallen in love with the Nordic lands.

The efficient railway network covers an area as far north as Alaska and the Arctic tundra of Canada and Siberia. And only in the train can one relax and admire the scenery or watch with interest as the local farmers, tradesmen, or children alight at a small station situated amidst some remote mountains.

This book gives valuable information for tourists wishing to visit Oslo, Stockholm, Trondheim, Kiruna or Rovaniemi in Finnish Lapland.

There is also detailed information on the famous BERGEN RAILWAY and the scenic FLAM RAILWAY, which are probably two of the most beautiful lines in the world.

HAPPY JOURNEY — *'BON VOYAGE'*

Der er en lykke i livet
Som ikke vendes til lede,
Det at du gleder en annen
Det er den eneste glede

Arnulf Overland

. . . . true happiness can only be found by making others happy.

LIST OF CONTENTS

THE RAILWAYS OF THE SCANDINAVIAN LANDS.

The growth of the railways in Scandinavia was slow, owing to the great distances between centres of population and industry, difficult physical conditions, and extreme climatical conditions.

All of the four Scandinavian lands have State owned railways and I have gained great pleasure and a delightful variety of experiences travelling thousands of miles by train, from the fertile farmlands of Skane in the south of Sweden, to the town of Rovaniemi in Finnish Lapland, and Narvik and Kiruna, well north of the Arctic circle. And I have seen such splendour of wild and inspiring natural scenery, and met fascinating men and women of all types and occupations.

If one has the time and inclination, there is no finer way of travelling in the Northern lands and really getting to know the people.

Work on the first line in Finland, Helsinki to Hameenlinna commenced in 1858 and the line was opened in 1862, thus linking the Hame district with the Gulf of Finland. By 1870 the Lahti-Viipuri-St. Petersburg line was completed, and the success of these railways encouraged extensions during the next 3 decades.

Norway had many obstacles to overcome, but hard work and determination have worked miracles in this land of great contrasts and superb scenery. Robert Stevenson acted as chief engineer for the first line, built by British capital, from Oslo to Eidsvoll, a distance of 42 miles.

The railway pattern consists essentially of lines radiating out from Oslo, to Stavanger, to Bergen, in a westerly direction, northwards to Trondheim and Bodo, eastwards to Stockholm, and southwards to Gothenburg and Copenhagen. Superimposed on this radial pattern, which has been provided at great cost, are spur lines which extend either into the valleys, as at Fagernes and Storlien, or to ports, such as Arendal and Andalsnes, which are off the main routes. The railways are not yet all linked together, and there are a few isolated lines which

1

run from various ports and are chiefly concerned with the mining and transportation of minerals.

It was a tremendous problem to connect the busy port of Bergen to Oslo the capital, and before the railhead at Voss could advance the best route had to be firmly determined. The choice lay between 1. from Voss to Laerdal and then either by Steinberg and Hallingdal or by Filefeld and Valdres. 2. From Voss to Eidfjord and south of the Hardanger glacier into Hallingdal or Numedal or over the Hardanger Vidda into Telemark, or 3. From Voss by the route actually adopted along Raundal and Hallingdal.

This was an epic railway construction and the section across the fjell took from 1894 until 1907 to build, largely because of the problem of cutting the tunnel of Gravehals, 17,427 ft. (5,309m) through granite. Workmen had to toil through the long extremely cold Winter months and endure terrific wind velocities. Often drifting snow choked the tunnel mouths so that the rock debris could not be cleared. At first Italian tunnelers were employed, but as they were unable to withstand the rigours of Winter, they were replaced by Norwegians.

On this line between Bergen and Oslo there are 184 tunnels with a total length of about 24 miles (38 km.). The summit of this line, 4,267 ft (1,300m), compares with 4,494 ft. (1,370m) at the Brenner pass and 4,244 ft. (1,294m) on the Mount Cenis route which are over 15 degrees of latitude further south and enjoy a much milder climate with much shorter winters.

Some of the lines are highly popular by tourists from all parts of Europe, especially the famous Flam line. This line descends 2,837 ft. (805m) from Myrdal to Flam by a series of great spirals in a mere 16 miles (24 km).

The Nordland line extends from Trondhein to Bodo, a distance of about 450 miles, about 13 hours by train, as there are many tunnels and mountainous areas to be crossed, and only in 1947 did the line extend as far as the Arctic circle.

The majority of ports on the south coast are served by the Sorlandsbanen. This extends in a huge arc, firstly in a south-westerly direction towards Kristiansand, and then northwards towards Stavanger. There are several side lines serving some of the more important ports, such as Arendal, Larvik, and Kragero, and there are some spectacular views of the Gausta mountain., the highest mountain south of the Hardanger range.

SWEDEN

The great mileage of railway compared with area in Sweden is largely due to the more developed areas of southern and central Sweden, and if the vast and rather barren Norrland is excluded the figure is even higher. The length of railway per inhabitant is the highest in Europe and the total distance is in the region of 10,500 miles (17,000 km).

The railway system developed rather late. In the first half of the last century rails were laid for horse-drawn wagons in the Bergslagen district. And the first modern railway was the British owned track of 11 miles, from Arboga to Orebro, in 1856.

The Riksdag decided in 1855 to build on a large scale, and work was started near Gothenburg, in 6 years 438 miles were completed, from Gothenburg to Stockholm, and from Malmo to Liatorp. British capital helped boost rapid expansion, in 1870 the first railway in Norrland was opened, and the following 50 years brought vigorous development. The inland railway from Kristinehamn in Varmland to Gallivare in Lapland was opened in sections over 26 years, being completed in 1937. The last line to have been built was from Ulricehamn to Jonkoping. There are only a few tunnels, as the gradients are generally very gradual, unlike Norway. But bridge building was quite a formidable task, for many of the rivers flowing into the Gulf of Bothnia, such as the Ume, Pite, Angerman, and Ore, are wide in their lower reaches. From Boden to Langsele, a distance of 311 miles (498 km) there are several large bridges.

DENMARK

Here the development was fairly simple, for the land is fairly level, and only the construction of long bridges needed extra effort. The first railway track 20 miles, from Copenhagen to Roskilde, took place in 1847. Slowly more lines were constructed, chiefly to help with the export of grain and foodstuffs, as at the town of Struer, on the Limfjord. Building extremely long bridges, to save time with car ferries, happened in the thirties. The Little Belt Bridge, 2,953 ft. (900m) and the Storstrom Bridge 10,499 ft. (3,200m) in 1937, has saved much time for transport.

As Denmark consists of several large islands, the train ferries are of vital importance to the general economy, and also connect Denmark to Sweden and Germany in a most efficient manner. The islands of Mors and Aero, which are without railways, can receive road vehicles by ferry to avoid rehandling costs. A bridge has also been planned across the Oresund sound, to connect Denmark to Sweden.

FINLAND.

Travelling by train in Finland is not only highly enjoyable, it is the perfect way of exploring this wild and rugged Northern land, of vast forests and ten thousand lakes. There are over 3,000 miles of track, covering the coastline and ports of the Gulf of Finland and the Gulf of Bothnia. Inland an excellent network links the majority of towns of reasonable size and importance, such as Imatra and Joensuu, on the Soviet border, and Jyvaskyla and Kajaani, in the

4

very heart of the forested interior.

And Finland is unique in that one can combine travel by rail and steamer on the Saimaa and Paijanne lakes. How fascinating it is to travel by night at Midsummer and watch a multitude of celebrations where the twilight of the light evenings turns into the warm crimson of the beckoning dawn. And the express train from Helsinki can take one the whole way to Rovaniemi, in the heart of Lapland, the last wilderness in Northern Europe. Here one can experience the indescribable splendour of Autumn, when the trees of the Arctic forests are ablaze of colour. This season is know as 'Ruska' by the Finns, who love nature and open-air exercise and recreation.

Often the forests completely surround the smaller stations, and sometimes the stations are situated by a deep blue lake. For those who love train travel, nature, and meeting friendly people, Finland offers great opportunities.

THE RAILWAYS OF NORWAY.

Many of us have found lasting happiness and enjoyment in making numerous journeys by train, in England or abroad. I have been fortunate in having the opportunity to travel by train in many parts of Europe, from Cornwall, in the far west of England, to Moscow in Eastern Europe, and from Southern Germany and Austria to Rovaniemi on the Arctic Circle in Northern Finland, just immediately south of the Tundra, where snow lies over half the year.

And yet the Norwegain State Railways have given me the greatest happiness of all. I have travelled countless thousands of miles on their fascinating routes, relaxed in comfort on their fast and modern trains, made new friends on countless occasions, and found a thousand delights in the grandeur of the Norwegian landscape. For Norway is a land of great contrasts, high mountains where only mosses and grass grow during the short Summers, and sheltered verdant valleys where the heat of a Summer's day is just like being in the tropics.

Each district of Norway is completely different, the extreme South with mild Winters and warm Summers, the West Coast with heavy rainfall and a climate similar to Northern Scotland, the Northern Area, with long, cold Winters, and short Summers, and the Eastern region, with reliable, hot Summers, and extremely cold, Winters.

5

TO TRAVEL BY TRAIN IN NORWAY IS TO DISCOVER NORWAY.

Norway in many aspects is unique, being the most Northern civilised land in the World, a land of high mountains and a rugged landscape seldom to be found elsewhere. It is a land of long Summer days, with eternal light in the Northern part, and long, dark Winter nights.

One factor alone makes this land of splendour fit for human, plant, and animal vegetation, and this is the warming influence of the Gulf Stream, which washes her far flung shores and mighty fjiords, from Lindesnes in the South, to the North Cape, well above the Arctic circle. Many areas of Siberia and Canada, even further South than these two remote points, are in the Perma frost region.

And what a formidable challenge Norway has given the pioneers of Railway construction. High mountains, narrow winding valleys, rushing rivers, long fjiords, do not easily yield to the two bands of shining steel which join East and West, North and South, carrying heavy freight and passengers from as far away as Australia, New Zealand, Canada, and Japan. Spring, Summer, Autumn, and Winter, the powerful trains scale the high mountains, winding slowly up the valleys, crossing cascading waterfalls, and traversing many a long tunnel which have been blasted deep into the granite rocks. Forward, forward, the swiftly rotating wheels seems to beckon, in perfect rhythm, almost like a song of joy.

The sound of the wheels is like the music of Edvard Grieg, full of happiness and gratitude for the splendid scenery which continually surrounds us and changes on the journey, whether long or short.

We have to thank the enterprising British contractors under the strong and brilliant leadership of Robert Stephenson, and the spontaneous help and skilled co-operation of the Norwegian Government to the building of Norway's first railway project. This was the stretch of line between Oslo and Eidsvoll, in 1854.

It was George Stevenson who was the originator of Englands and the World's first railway in 1825, and it was his son who carried on his dedicated work in England and elsewhere.

Many keen rail enthusiasts, both in Norway and England, love to quote the journalist Gordon Young, who wrote in the 'Viking Lands' 1948.

In this land of mountains and fjiords the wonder is that there are not more railways, but that there are any at all. When you see the solid barriers of rock through which the railways must find a way, you feel that any less enterprising nation than the Norwegians would have decided that it was impossible to build a railway of any sort. Yet there the railway tracks are, and the trains are kept working even through the depths of Winter, with the aid of powerful snowploughs and wooden barriers to prevent the snow drifting over the line.

In relation to it's population, Norway takes pride of second place in Europe, while it's good neighbour Sweden comes first. And yet if we look at our railways in relation to the total land area, Norway is the last place. This clearly indicates the small population that lives in a relatively large country, and this too makes the conditions even more unfavourable for an efficient and profitable railway system.

Norway has a total of 4,300 kilometers (Approx. 2,850 miles) of single track railways, only a minute proportion are double tracks, chiefly in the vicinity of Oslo and Drammen, where the density of traffic is extremely high. And by far the greatest proportion of lines are in Southern Norway, 82% are south of Trondhein. The Norwegian State Railways maintain a highly efficient fleet of buses to maintain contact between many towns and communities remote from the nearest station, for example, Andalsnes and Alesund, both on the mountainous coastal region of Sunnmore, an area of truly magnificent scenery. Amongst the mountains of Telemark and Trondheim area it is just the same friendly and reliable combination of bus and train travel.

When the building of Norway's first railway was begun in 1851, a newspaper wrote 'The conditions peculiar to Norway's land surface, it's singularly uninhabitable regions which in part lie so high above sea-level that they are either covered by snow the year round or give a foothold only to Tundra vegetation, make the extensive use of locomotive railways in this country impossible or unsuitable.'

Fifty years later the Ofot Railway between the border and Narvik opened for traffic. This extremely short yet highly important stretch of track covers rugged, lonely country about 230 kilometers north of the Artic circle. For a long time it was the World's northermost railway, and even today is the northernmost electrified line. Every day of the year, 20 trains, each loaded with over 3,000 tons of iron ore, are transporting their heavy and precious loads from the ore mines of Kiruna to the ice free port of Narvik.

On June 7, 1962, it was a joyous day for many Norwegians, when King Olav V opened the Nordland Railway which goes to the sea at Bodo — an unbroken rail connection between Oslo and Bodo, a distance of some 1,300 kilometers, about 800 miles, about as far as Penzance is from Inverness, the North of Scotland.

For the time being, this is the culmination of Norwegian Railway building which has taken place for over a century. And it can be truly stated that the construction of the Bergen Railway, and it's offshoot, the Flam Line, from Mydral to the Aurlandsfjord, are the highlights of pioneering.

The Bergen Line, which was opened by King Haakon in 1909, connects East and West Norway, and the most important connection between the capital of Oslo, and Bergen, also an important seaport and Norway's second largest town. It is 470 kilometers long (about 295 miles) and at it's highest point, just west of Finse, the highest station in Northern Europe, reaches 1,301 meters above sea level, approx. 4,300 feet high. It is also fascinating to note that each station, however small, has it's own altitude clearly written in meters for the benefit of the observant passenger.

In America and Switzerland the lines go even higher, but for a distance of 100 kilometers the track traverses a remote area devoid of trees, so harsh is the climate with short Summers. It was a daring venture that engineers and workers of great diversity and skills began at the turn of the century, with the marking out of the bed and the laying of the tracks. And this was on the very geographical roof of Norway, with spike and minedrill, sledgehammar and crowbar, spade and heavy wheel-barrow. It was a splendid and determined use of brain, muscle, and dynamite which made it a success. They dug the rail bed right into the very precipices of the mountain side, and built it up with great high walls with the mountain towering above and the deep fjord below.

They forced it farther over bridges and gigantic fill-ins, steadily away from the fjords and coastal settlements up through the valley and on to the high mountains, glistening with white snow and seemingly invincible. But hard work and determination conquered in the end.

The Bergen Railway is of engineering greatness and Norwegian genius. The writer Nils Kjaer was so enthusiastic and moved by this structural feat, that he wrote. ------ The mountain railway is our finest national achievement, especially as it was built by a nation so small. Each bridge, each snow fence, each tunnel is more remarkable than all our excavated Viking findings together. The mountain has, at last been

8

conquered. This forbidding wasteland, whose snow-fields scorn the sun and whose Summer is only a little light, whose Spring is confounded by the previous Winter, and is threatened by that to come, finally had to give way to the will of man. But even then it still arose in sudden and unexpected resistance. Snow drifts filled in the way, and on each stormy night the eternal conflict between man and nature is renewed.

The entire trip takes about 8 hours, and there are about 200 tunnels, 300 bridges, and about 28 kilometers of wooden snowbarriers, along it's total length of 470 kilometers. Indeed, from the wide windows you can clearly see a splendid panorama of Norway the Sublime, all in glorious technicolour. The Norwegians, by constant travel over this fascinating line, slowly discovered a vast, unspoilt open-air playground for skiers, ramblers, and sportsmen. And all along the line tourist hotels, youth hostels, and log cabins grew up in a beautiful way, and still blending with their natural background of mountains and valleys, forests, lakes, and rapidly flowing rivers and streams. People take it for granted that the trains will always run to the timetable. Few take time to think about the endless effort needed to keep the line open. This is also why the snow tunnels are so necessary. Finse is the headquarters of the snow clearers, and here between 30 and 40 men are stationed permanently to combat the snow. And even in short but delightful Summer their work is of vital importance, for only then can they tackle the necessary task of repairing the snow fences and tunnels.

In 1964 the Bergen Railway was completely electrified. Formerly the Gravehals tunnel was the longest tunnel, 5,311 meters long, the longest in Northern Europe, it was soon out-distanced by the 9,064 meters Kvineshei Tunnel between Kristiansand and Stavanger. Recently in 1973 the Lierasen tunnel was completed. It is 10,700 meters, and the longest North of the Alps, and now trains can speed from Oslo to Drammen in a mere 31 minutes. The tunnel through Mount Ulriken, just outside Bergen is the second most important.

And in 1970 the electrification of the Dovre Line, from Oslo to picturesque Trondheim, the historial Centre in former times, was completed. Already 57% of Norway's railways are electrically controlled.

A truly splendid feat in this rugged land of green valleys and snow-capped mountains.

THE DANISH STATE RAILWAYS.

The transport provided by the Danish State Railways can be classified into 3 main categories, firstly the long distance services, the series of branch lines, chiefly of local importance, and last but not least, the Copenhagen district electric system.

The long distance services are maintained chiefly by diesel locomotives and on a diminishing scale by steam locomotives. Besides the State Railways there is a fairly extensive but far less important network of private railways, the controlling interests being held by the local governments and the State.

It is interesting to note that the chief inland long distance trains serve the same connections as the main trunk roads. In addition there is a highly efficient network of fast secondary inland services, which, like most of the trains in the main network, are partly maintained by means of 'L' trains. These are short-stemmed diesel express trains (introduced in the 1930's), which like the international trains, are ferried across the Great Belt, the stretch of water seperating the two islands, Sjaelland and Funen.

A number of connections are maintained by means of ordinary express services, there is also a network of branch lines, which includes all the private railway sections. The last-named, with the exception of a few weekend and other special trains, do not run express services. The Copenhagen district system chiefly consists of a system electrified in the 1930's and since gradually extended (S - baner).

The international lines connect Denmark with Germany, and Sweden, and to a lesser extent, Norway, Poland, and Great Britian. Several excellent train services are run on the main inland sections.

Of the total number of passengers conveyed by the State Railways, approx. two-thirds are carried by the Copenhagen district electric system, and about 5 per cent are the motorists using the frequent

ferries between the main islands. These figures are slowly increasing, owing to the steady growth of Copenhagen's population and use of cars for everyday transport.

Outside greater Copenhagen there has been no new lines constructed, except for a section on the island of Lolland, as part of the new continental connection to Schleswig Holstein in Northern Germany.

A very extensive programme of modernisation and rationalization has been achieved, the gradual transition from steam to diesel. conversion

10

of signalling systems to automatic working, station improvements, and so on. New, faster ferries have reduced the travel times between many towns.

About half of the revenue of the State Railways is derived from passenger traffic, about a third from freight transport, and the remainder from car ferries, mail, and various coach services. The average distance of freight journeys is 208 kilometers (129 miles), while the average length of passenger journeys is a mere 29 kilometers (18 miles).

The seating capacity is approx. 104,000 and the freight load 217,000 tons. About 32 ferries and ships are owned by the State Railways. The principal ferry services are the Halskov - Knudshoved car ferry service and the Korsor - Nyborg rail and car ferry service, both across the Great Belt. The Elsinore - Halsingborg and Copenhagen - Malmo ferries make many everyday connections to Sweden, and the new Rodby - Puttgarden ferry speeds the connection between Germany and Denmark. The Gedser - Warnemunde service to the German Democratic Republic has been of minor importance since the war. As in Norway and Sweden, the railways still run at a small deficit, which is covered by the Government administration.

The Danish State Railways employ a staff of about 27,000 and of this the permanent staff is about 18,000. Of this number, about 1,100 are employed on coach services. The private railways employ 2,400, of these 1,300 are permanently employed.

PLEASANT DAY-TRIPS FROM COPENHAGEN

Copenhagen is an ideal centre for making short day trips. The journey to Odense takes about three hours and the ferry between Korsor and Nyborg, connecting the islands of Sjaelland and Fyn, takes about one hour. In Odense one has time to explore the narrow, cobbled streets and visit the home of Hans Christian Andersen, who by his lovable writing, gave joy to children all over the world. The train museum is a "must" for all train lovers. A longer trip can be made to Aarhus with its wonderful museum of old houses.

Only one hour from Copenhagen is Helsingor with Kronberg castle. It is Elsinore in Shakespeare's "Hamlet".

At Hillerod, just 21 miles from the capital, and easily reached by local commuter train, is Frederiksborg castle, a treasure of artistic beauty and Danish culture and history. Worth a visit too is the Viking ship museum at Roskilde.

Across the Oresund Sound in Sweden is Malmo, a very good town to buy Swedish glassware and quality souvenirs.

THE BERGEN RAILWAY.

A splendid Autumn journey from Oslo to Bergen.

Early one October morning I awoke. The sky was a deep blue,
stretching into the pale purple hue of the distant horizon. On the
ground was a keen frost, sparking white in the first early rays of
the brilliant sun. From the wide windows of the Haraldsheim Youth
Hostel, high up on the slopes of Grefsen, a suburb of Oslo, I had a
magnificent view over the town below, already bustling with activity
as cars sped towards the factories and offices, the calm azure waters
of the Oslo Fjord, and the distant chain of mountains to the North
and West. Quite near were the densely wooded slopes of the
Holmenkollen mountain, with the cluster of residential areas on it's
lower slopes.

It was time to leave Oslo, the fascinating capital of that splendid land,
Norway, and return to England. And how many happy memories it
brought me, warm Summer days, long light evenings, wonderful
friendships, easy days and hard days, working in gardens, and making
journeys by train, car, and foot. Only the previous evening I had
visited the National Theatre, and greatly enjoyed a humorous play by
Ludvig Holberg, Den Stundenlose.

Saying goodbye to friends at the hostel, and Mr. and Mrs. Maehlum,
who lived nearby, I lifted my heavy rucksack and descended the
steep grassy slope leading to the tram stop. It was with a mixture of
excitement and feeling of longing to return as Haraldsheim slowly
became smaller until it merged with a multitude of other buildings in
it's near vicinity.

The tram was packed with smartly dressed office workers, and
students of all ages, many had hurried to catch the tram at the very
last minute. The very walls of the high blocks and factories seemed to
echo and enlarge the noise of cars, lorries and buses, while overhead a

12

large plane slowly descended prior to landing at the Fornebu airport.
At last the overloaded tram came to a grinding halt and spewed out it's
occupants into the busy streets joining the Karl Johansgaten and the
Ostbanen, the main station.

And it was not long before the electric train was swiftly climbing towards
the Northern suburbs of this beautiful city. I caught a distant glimpse of
Haraldsheim Youth Hostel, below the high slopes of the Grefsenkollen
hill, and passed the calm waters of Lake Mariedalsvannet. Now the train
winded through the forested hills of Nordmarka, a quiet, unspoilt area
and a paradise for lovers of the open-air. All around reigned peace and
calm, it seemed strange to visualise so much natural beauty so near a
rapidly expanding town of industry and administration.

Near the junction of Roa there was a fine view of the Jaeren area, well
known for it's well kept farmsteads and small hillside huts, known as
'Saeter '. These huts were used for hillside grazing of cattle and sheep,
and now are often turned into holiday cottages for city people. At
Honefoss a brief halt was made, and passengers from Drammen and the
Sorlandsbanen in the extreme South of Norway alighted before the
train quickly gained speed in a smooth and effortless manner.

By now the sun was quite warm, and there were only pockets of frost
on the lower valley slopes. Happy and relaxed, I sat back and admired
the every-changing scenery, before dozing off for a few brief minutes.
One of the joys of travel by train is that one never has to worry about
traffic queues or road accidents, and one generally arrives on time, wind
or rain, sun or snow. After passing through the Soknedal, the mile long
tunnel was traversed, and we were in the famous long winding
Hallingdal valley, with it's long Kroderen lake.

What a splendid morning it was, the waters of the lake sparkled like
diamonds, and to the West the first snows of the Autumn were on the
high mountain slopes near Norjefjell.

The Hallingdal valley was adorned in all her Autumn glory, the tall,
dark forms of the pine and fir trees contrasted to the bright colours
of the deciduous tress. And the inland lakes, large and small,
reflected the delicate hues of the blue and purple skies and the
immediate surroundings.

Besides each waterway the brilliantly arrayed trees bend gently over as
though in admiration of their clearly reflected images. Even the small,
insignificant grasses and willows by the shores catch the light hearted
spirit and form an almost horizontal line to the colours of the forests
which merge into the bluish horizon.

No gifted and highly talented painter could portray every shade and colour so delicate and varied. And no brilliantly alert actor could portray Autumn in all it's slowly changing colour.

At Nesbyen a few Norwegian families from Oslo hurried along the platform, to catch a local bus to their cozy huts in the vicinity. At Gol station there was much activity, for this community is an important centre for the Hallingdal and roads leading to the Valdres mountains, and Hemsedal leading to the mighty Sogne fjord, which stretches a hundred miles from the West Coast to the interior, and is the longest fjord in Norway. The Hardanger and Nordfjord are the next largest fjords, and all are a great attraction to tourists from all corners of the World.

The train made a lengthy halt at Al, and I had time to join a rather impatient queue and enjoyed some excellent coffee at the station cafeteria. I almost pity those waitresses who do all they can to help the thirsty passengers who suddenly descend on them from a packed train. The line from Bergen to Oslo has only a single track, owing to the high cost of construction in mountainous terrain. At several of the stations the line becomes double track, to allow a train to pass in the opposite direction.

Al is almost exactly half way between Oslo and Bergen, and in former times the trains were changed here. A more powerful engine was used from Al over the high Hardanger mountain plateau, as here the gradients are far steeper.

In this quiet town, surrounded by deeply wooded hills live two friends of mine, Esther and Ivar, in a friendly wooden house. They are both teachers at the local school, Ivar specialises in metal work and carpentry, Esther teaches English, history, and general subjects. I am indeed grateful for their hospitality and kindness.

After leaving Al the terrain took on a more rugged nature, and soon the forests and farmsteads of the Hallingdal gave way to the mountains. How attractive the mountain resort of Geilo looked, a cheerful porter from the nearby Holms hotel helped an elderly man with his luggage, I almost envied him, relaxing at such a splendid resort with fine vistas over the mountains and air like wine.

As the train climbed even higher the pine trees slowly disappeared and gave way to dwarf birches, their barks were gleaming like silver in the bright sunshine. There is perhaps no tree so graceful as the birch, it has a beauty of it's own both in Winter and Summer, almost like a ballet dancer.

14

From the wide window of the train I glanced out and saw the rushing streams and cascades of numerous waterfalls, the water had a bluish colour, owing to it's glacial origin. Finse station is well over 4,000 ft., and there was already thick snow just below the 6,000 Hardanger glacier. Scott of the Antarctic trained here before his courageous venture to the South Pole.

How wild and challenging the landscape looked, drifts of snow quite near the track, and the whole landscape a strange mixture of white snow, black rocks, rushing streams almost with a song of joy conveyed in their swiftly running waters, and the multitude of lakes, blue, calm and serene.

At Taugevann, altitude 1,300 meters (4,260 ft.) the highest point was reached, it was almost like a clearly marked line parting East and West Norway, and I noticed the mountain streams were flowing in a Westerly direction. The sun was much lower in the sky, and only the higher fells were bathed in brilliant sunshine.

There were so many snowscreens that at times it was almost impossible to see much from the slowly descending train. But these are of vital importance to keep the line open throughout the severe Winters. The Station at Finse has about 30 men who are occupied full time to keep the line clear in the Winter, and repair the track and snow screens during the brief Summer.

At Hallingskeid the station is entirely under cover, for there are many avalanches at this remote spot, and enterprising railway engineers have built the station right into the mountain side. The next stop is Myrdal, and just before we arrive there is a magnificient view on the right of the Flam valley and the electric railway. The conductor makes the announcement over the train's loudspeaker system so that no one will miss this breathtaking vista.

The Flam Line passes through 20 tunnels with a total length of 3.7 miles and at the finest views the train slows down or makes a brief halt to enable passengers to enjoy their journey as much as possible. For the first mile or two the Flam Line runs through a series of snow sheds almost parallel to the track of the Bergen Line, and at Vatnahalsen the view over the steeply sloping Flam valley with the high surrounding mountains capped by perpetual snow, has to be seen to be believed. And between Kjosfossen and Bakli the train crosses a long embankment, where swift waters cascade from ledge to ledge below with untamed majesty.

The last thousand feet descent from the Myrdal mountains to the level of the Aurlands fjord is negotiated by a reverse tunnel so that in all the line runs at five levels within a point to point distance of 0.6 mile.

Before entering the longest tunnel, Nali 1,476 yards long, the most spectacular scenery is passed. While the train stands at the fourth level, the other three levels of the line can be seen, and also the steep road which climbs Myrdal mountain in 21 turns. Finally at Hareina the valley widens out, and here are well kept farmsteads and the old church of Flam. The Flam station is at the head of the Aurlandsfjord, which joins the Sognefjord, over 100 miles in length, Norway's longest, and one of the most scenic. The growth here is very luxuriant, with oaks, sycamamores, and beech trees, and smiling orchards of plum, pear, and apple, thanks to the moist and mild climate of the sheltered valley.

The brakes had to be applied as the train descended through the Gravahalstunnel, and Upsete I immediately noticed how steep the mountains were, for the Western part of the mountain chain is much steeper than the Eastern part. Here too, the rainfall is much heavier as the rain bearing Westerly winds precipitate most of their load on the Western slopes. And the Winters are less severe than further East. At Mjofjell the very first dwarf birches made a welcome appearance, and soon after were fine specimens of pines. Lower down the line were splendid forests of pine and spruce, a deep green colour in the early twilight, while cattle grazed peacefully in the verdant valleys.

At the mountain resort of Voss, which is also an important route centre, a lengthy halt was made. This delightful mountain town, with its nearby Lake Vossevangen was a marked contrast in it's green and gentle surroundings, yet only a few minutes walk takes one to mountain slopes.

Voss brings back many happily memories of travel in Norway the Sublime. I recollect so vividly when I hiked to Bergen from Oslo. It was the end of May, and owing to deep snow still remaining over the road on the Hardanger plateau, took the train from Geilo to Voss.

Early in the morning I left Voss, took a car lift to Granvin, and walked several miles across lonely mountains until I reached the Hardanger Fjord. The sky was a bright blue, the fjord calm and shimmering in the warm sunshine. Apple trees in the orchards were in full bloom, the houses painted in bright colours, while overhead the snow on the Folgefonn mountain was a dazzling white. It was just like the famous painting 'Brudeferd i Hardanger' 'The Bridal Journey' by Tidemand and Gude, two Norwegian portrait and landscape painters who worked together with infinite patience to create this masterpiece.

Between Bulken and Dale the train passed through a narrow wild valley with almost vertical mountains on both sides. There were several scattered farmsteads and I noticed many of the children wave as the train passed by. We were once again in the area of the Western Fjords, and after leaving Arna, we passed through the Ulriken tunnel, which is the longest on this route, 7,660 meters, about 5 miles long.

And so Bergen came into sight, and the friendly driver spoke over the loudspeaker, thanking us for our attention, and saying he hoped we thoroughly enjoyed the long, scenic journey. He spoke clearly in Norwegian and English, and the Norwegians have voices which reminds one of the freshness of the mountains and the echo of the waterfalls.

How refreshing it was to alight and walk along the long platform, breathing in the clear, crisp air. I bought a few postcards at the station kiosk, before climbing on a rather overladen bus going in the direction of the Montana Youth Hostel. How overjoyed I was to meet the warden and his wife, John and Synnove.

They made me some delicious sandwiches and tea, and from the lounge the whole town could be seen below. Ten thousand street lights stretched out from the centre like a string of pearls, what an unforgettable sight it was.

What a splendid journey it had been, so much beauty and contrast, so many unexpected surprises, and everlasting memories. Throughout the length and breadth of Norway, nothing can equal or excel the journey on the Bergen Line Railway.

It was a Blessing Divine in Norway The Sublime.

ANCIENT AND MODERN. TRAIN AT SAVONLINNA, NEAR SOVIET FRONTIER, IN BACKGROUND OLAVINLINNA THE LARGEST MEDIEVAL FORTRESS IN SCANDINAVIA.

17

THE DOVRE LINE.

The important railway line which connects Oslo, Norway's thriving and modern capital and chief seaport, to Trondheim, the old capital of Norway, a town of great historic beauty and delightful old World charm.

The whole journey offers splendid contrasts of smiling meadows, deep green valleys, many lakes, rushing rivers and waterfalls and snow-capped peaks. If you have the time, it is a journey to be well recommended.

The initial part of the journey passes through the built-up area of Oslo's outskirts, and many large industrial sites. We soon pass through an area rich in forests and everywhere are numerous high hills. The track goes through the region which seperates Nordmarka and Ostmarka, where many of the Oslo citizens enjoy quiet relaxation, walking and swimming in the Summer, and skiing during the dry, healthy Winters.

Soon we are in the Romerike province, gently undulating land interspersed by pine and spruce forests and low hilly outcrops. This is a splendid farming land, rich and fertile, with severe Winters, and warm, dry and sunny Summers, and here grow crops in abundance. In ancient times lived many of the Norwegian Vikings, and at Raknehavgen in Ullensaker is one of Norway's oldest and largest burial mounds.

This, for all train-lovers, is also a region of tradition, for in 1854, thanks to the co-operation between the Norwegians and Robert Stevenson, the son of the famous George Stevenson, the first line between Oslo and Eidsvoll was put into use for the public.

Eidsvoll is of long-lasting historical significance, for in former times it was the meeting point for the Eidsivating, the local parliament for Eastern Norway, and here too was a meeting to give fresh laws and administration after the seperation from Danish authority. It was May 17th, 1814. It is situated only 5 kilometers from the small and friendly railway station, the old government building is on the main road from Oslo, just the place to visit for a true lover of Norwegian Democracy and progress.

At Minnesundet, the extreme southern point of Lake Mjøsa, can be clearly seen the 'Skibnader', Norway's oldest, and only remaining paddle-steamer.

Evern since 1856 it has sailed each Summer between Hamar and Lillehammar., bringing happiness to young and old and a delight to tourists from many nations.

Mjøsa is Norway's largest lake, with a surface area of 360 square kilometers, and on it's western shores steep, wooded hills rise steeply to a mountain chain called Skreia, rising to 850 meters (approx. 2,650 ft.). The railway line goes for many miles quite close to the shores, and the farms of Hedemark are some of the most extensive in the whole of Norway.

The long Summer evenings, the light and shade on the hills and surface of the lake, and the splendour of the sunsets have to be seen to be believed.

> 'And, when night in falling
> Brings as dreams to Earth'.

Over the loudspeaker, the friendly voice of the driver announces, in Norwegian and perfect English — 'Attention please, all passengers, the next stop is Hamar, please alight for platform on left side.' How thoughtful, helping the passenger to collect his odds and ends 3 or 4 minutes before arriving at his destination. What a pity British Rail does not copy this splendid idea. Even the second class has reclining seats, coat hangers, and clean linen headrests which are always replaced after each journey.

Hamar, with a thriving textile industry, steel foundry, timber and wood processing factory, is also a vital road and rail centre. The town also boasts of technical and occupational schools, and is sometimes called the 'Schooltown'.

This town, so far away from my small town on the South Coast of England, is very near and dear to me, strange as it may seem. When the Nazis came to power, a rather insignificant young German left his home-land helped by a kindly fisherman from Schleswig Holstein to Denmark. Long before the war, he had been to the Scandinavian lands, and had grown to love and respect their democracy, love of freedom of expression, and individualistic attitude, found in both their leaders and hard working farmers and fishermen.

So he returned once again to his beloved Norway, and worked for two years as a reporter for the 'Arbeiderbladet', a progressive Socialist news-paper in Oslo. When Norway was invaded, he was interned by the Germans for a short time. Luckily they believed he was a student who spoke German

19

very fluently, and he was later able to enter Sweden as a refugee for the second time.

Willy Brandt had therefore, in a space of few years, acquired three different nationalities, first Norwegian, then Swedish, and later German. While the decisive battles for Moscow, Stalingrad, and Kursk were being fought on Soviet soil he was already formulating a plan for reconciliation between the Germans and Russians, as a refugee in Stockholm.

His attractive and charming wife is a friendly, homely Norwegian from Hamar, and their home in Berlin is furnished in the Traditional Norwegian style.

Willy Brandt has spent a lifetime in the service of Peace and Humanity. His love of Human Dignity extends not just to Norwegians, Danes, Swedes, and Germans, but to a multitude of nations throughout the World. 'He is a portrait of a humble and noble German', I say to myself, everytime I glimpse his smiling face in a paper or magazine.

Anyone, who not only loves Peace, but strives, with tireless energy and patient devotion for Peace, is to be sincerely admired in every way possible.

Lake Mjøsa has it's largest breadth near Hamar, further North it narrows almost to the width of a large river, and at Lillehammar a road bridge connects the East side to the prosperous farming area on the West side.

Lillehammar, the next most important stop, is a very popular mountain resort, both in Winter and Summer, and has a healthy, dry climate. It is only a few kilometers to the idyllic areas to the East, and the valleys and mountains to the North and West.

At Maihaugen are the Sandvig historical and folk-lore collections named after their founder, Anders Sandvig. With a total of over a hundred buildings, of all shapes and sizes, chiefly from the Gudbrandsdalen, it is the biggest in Norway, and unique from others in Europe.

Here, in delightfully natural surroundings, is a Stavechurch from the eleventh century, an old farmstead of 26 houses, a saeter collection, and many other houses. And a museum depicts how 50 different types of workers carried on their skills long ago.

Lillehammer is the gateway to the Gudbrandsdalen, and already at Faberg we pass the first neighbouring side valley at Gausdal. At Aulestad, the poet and author, Bjornstjerne Bjornson lived and worked. Apart from receiving the Nobel Prize, he also composed the Norwegian National Anthem.

The Gudbrandsdalen has many large farms, some of them have as many as

20 or 30 buildings, for storing the crops, hay, and farm workers with their families. The Eastern side has most of the farming settlements, as here there is more sun, and less frost and snow-cover than the West-side.

Lower down the valley is very gradual, and the river Lagen flows very slowly, North of Tretten is the Lake Losna. Further on, after Hundorp, the valley is rather steeper, and to the East and West is the mountain chain of the Valdres and Jotunheimen.

Vinstra, Sjoa, and Otta are named after the three rivers which give the river Lagen much of it's supply.

These rivers flow from the high fjells of the Jotunheimen, and their wide valleys give access to the manificent nature which are a source of inspiration for those who hike on the mountains. At Vinstra is the burial site of Per Gynt, and this great farmer from Fron in Gudbrandsdalen was the title given to a play by Henrik Ibsen.

From Otta is a road just North of the Jotunheimen to the province of Vestlandet, with the splendour of the fjords, Geiranger and Stryn, near Jostedalsbreen, Norway's largest glacier. Further South from the Jotunheimen the multitude of smaller fjords joining the Sognefjord give great happiness to the multitude of tourists who are fortunate to visit this region of scenic beauty.

We pass Sel, known from the gifted writer and Nobel Prize winner Sigrid Undset's novel of the Middle Ages 'Kristin Lavransdatter.
At this point the valley rises very steeply, and the railway winds in a great arc of a circle to overcome the steep rise of the terrain. After a brief halt at Dovre, we arrive at Dombas, which has a splendid situ ation, being surrounded by vast tracts of pine woods and high mountains, with the Dovrefjell to the North.

Formerly the train used to stay for some considerable time at Dombas, and I used to enjoy some light refreshments here, now the trains have been speeded up, this seems rather a pity, at least for a traveller who wishes to know even more of the fascinating land. From Dombas one can take the branch line to Andalsnes and the scenic Romsdal valley with it's surrounding massive mountains.

After leaving Dombas we come to the highest mountains on this long and highly beautiful journey to historical Trondheim.

The gradient is so steep as the train passes through the Gronbogen and shortly reaches Fokstua, 912 meters high, about 3,000 ft. above sea level. This is just above the tree line, but there is abundant alpine flora and bird-life, and a large piece of land has been protected as a Nature Reserve. The Norwegian Nature Conservation Society is doing much to preserve Nature and promote interest and progress in it's conservation.

This has, in it's turn influenced many idealists to also take action on their behalf.

Hjerkinn is the highest station on the route, 1,017 meters, about 3,300 ft. Proceeding on our way, the Snohetta mountain 2,286m. dominates the range of mountains towards the West, while to the Northeast is the Knutsho, over 1,700 meters. At Fokstua, Hjerkinn and Kungsvoll are old mountain huts, which were probably built by King Oystein in the 12th century.

This is the part of the journey I always love, the feeling of exhilaration and complete freedom as the train slowly descends in a Northerly direction, flanked by high mountains both to the West and East. Such beauty and grandeur, unspoilt by civilisation and so-called industrial progress.

Between Kongsvoll and Drivstua the railway goes through a thousand meter long tunnel under the Hogsnytafjellet, and just afterwards another tunnel, Hesteykrubben. Through this splendid mountain area went the old pilgrims way, high up above the rushing river Driva, cascading here and there in high waterfalls. The brakes have to be applied strongly as the descent into the upper Drivdal valley is quite rapid.

Near Oppdal, the River Driva turns towards the West, and flows through Sunndalen to the coast near Sunndalsora. For travel by bus or car, this journey to the coast and Kristiansund is to be highly recommended.

This region has huge forests of pine, spruce, and fir, and the province of Trondelag plays a vital role in timber production, both for home use and export. We continue through the Soknedal valley and stop at Storen, and this station connects with the Roros line, the older of the two lines connecting Oslo to Trondheim.

The very last stretch of the journey is through level and fertile agricultural land near the Gaudal river. We leave the Gaudal and the last 5 Kilometers hug the slopes of the Nidda river to reach our destination by the early evening.

Trondheim has a station which is modern, light and warm, as the entrance has automatic doors and the adjoining walls are of reinforced glass. From here there are frequent trains to Bodo in the North, Storlien on the Swedish Frontier and Stockholm, and Roros and eastern Norway.

Indeed, the station is so well equipped, I often take a stroll in the evening, just to watch the numerous passengers and tourists come and go.

In high spirits, I walked to the bus which was to take me to the Youth hostel. It was just like coming home, entering the hostel, and receiving a warm welcome and radiant smile from the warden, Rolf, and his industrious wife, Inger. And how their two sons Peter and Gunnar had grown since last year.

The sun was low on the Western horizon, as I joined my true friends for a delicious evening meal. The waters of the Trondheim fjord, calm and blue under a clear sky, took on a different hue as the sun set, like a crimson globe, under the dark outline of the mountains surrounding the fjord.

How grateful I was, as I thought of the magnificent scenery I had seen that day, the thoughts of all the work and skill required to build the railway across the high mountains, and most of all, the strong and lasting friendship of true Norwegian friends.

For true friendship is international
and unites the Human Race.

One blazing hot morning, towards the end of May, I left the bustling station of Oslo Ostbanen, and began the long train journey to Andalsnes. It is a highly enjoyable experience to travel from Dombas, high up in the Dovre mountains, to the green and fertile plain near the Isfjord, where the small coastal town of Andalsnes bids the traveller from afar a hearty welcome.

The track from Dombas at first went in a Northerly direction, and then slowly curved towards the West, passing through deep forests of mountain pine, their trunks a deep brownish red, almost like a burning fire in the bright sunshine. Soon we pass over the Jora bridge, spanning the Jora river.

At Lesja, A typical mountain settlement, the train made a welcome halt, and I noticed farmers were busy cutting back stubble and planting potatoes. How I love to watch people of all nations busy at work, for even tedious or menial work has a noble effect on mankind, for by honest work we help each other and improve our lives in every way. The train follows the Northern side of the valley, and we have a fine panoramic view over the Kjolenfjellene mountains on the Southern side. Most of the houses are arranged in groups, and generally are typical of the mountain region, low and rather old-fashioned. Strangely enough, this region has a very low annual rainfall, and the growing season is often too dry.

Further West the Kjolenfejellene mountains are followed by Mount Tverrfjell, which is much steeper, almost forming an immediate transition from the East to the Western Norwegian landscape. Near the single track, Lake Lesjaskogsvatn forms a watershed between East and west, and from here rivers flow in opposite directions. From Lillehammar the train had followed closely the River Lagan, and now we were to spend most of the time near the River Rauma as far as the coast.

At Bjorli the train passed through low woods of pine and birch and on either side a series of high wooden fences had been constructed to protect the line from heavy falls of snow. St. Olav is said to have passed this way on his long trek in 1028, when he was forced to leave Valldal in Gudbrandsdalen., and flee from Norway. Immediately after we leave Bjorli we say farewell to Eastern Norway and are made welcome to the inspiring and fascinating grandeur of Western Norway.

In the distance we see the ranges of the Romsdal Alps, Donntind Kaldskrtind, and Venjetindene, and we are soon entering the upper valley of the Romsdal valley. Borja is the mountain which marks the entrance to the Romsdal valley, and is very near the railway, on the Western side.

It is a splendid spectacle to watch the cascades of streams and water-falls which often fall vertically for several hundred feet, fed by the eternal snow of the upper slopes. The Rauma River races on, tumbling over steep precipices and pounding against the rock strewn bolders of deep ravines.

Then came a steep descent, passing the mile long Staven tunnel, which makes a complete turn inside the mountain. When the train emerged from the tunnel it continued in the opposite direction, immediately below the line above. I had a wonderful view of the Verma Falls, which plunge vertically 1,250 feet from the cliff top. Again the train entered the mountain, into the Kylling reverse tunnel, which makes a m assive gradual curve within the mountain and as the train left the long tunnel, it passed over the Kylling bridge, and I saw the river Rauma 200 feet below, thundering and foaming through a narrow gorge.

I looked up, and saw the railway line at 2 levels above me, it had traversed five miles in this double curve to bring it a mere 330 feet lower down in the valley. The valley slowly widened and became almost

24

level, and the river flowed at a more gentle pace. I had to strain my neck to view some of the higher summits, and from dizzy heights the waterfalls streamed down like gleaming silver strands. This valley was so green and fertile, and very carefully cultivated.

For centuries the farming population had lived and worked in this remote valley, working from dawn to dusk during the short Summer, and during the Wintertime, working with tapestry,weaving, and carpentry.

To my left soared the Trolltindene peaks, so steep that no snow ever lies on their slopes, which are completely devoid of vegetation. Here too, is the highest vertical rock face in Europe, Trollvegen, the precipice is over 3,000 ft. in height, and reaches out to the top of Trollryg gen, over 6,000 ft. high.

At Marstein station the nearby mountain peaks are so high that no sun reaches the valley for the 5 shortest months. And at Romsdal station we reach the wide plain of the lower reaches of the Romsdal valley, and the superb view of the lofty Romsdalhorn peak is something not to be missed. Further on we have a wide panorama of Isterdalen, with the Isterdalsfjellene, with their gleaming white summits, Dronningen, Kongen, and Bispen.

And so we reached Andalsnes, a town of a mere two or three thousand inhabitants, at the point where sea meets the mountains in a remarkable contrast. Even the station and it's surroundings had a fascination rather unique. It had a small and neat flower-garden, and a row of tall chestnut trees, their leaves looking so green and fresh in the bright sunshine.

I walked along the quiet streets which had only a little traffic, and even the drivers drove at a leasurely pace. Often the roads were lined with tall and slender birch trees, their bright green leaves swayed gently in a cool breeze coming off the calm waters of the Isfjord. The apple orchards were in full blossom, and both the houses and gardens were bright and gay, it was almost like a scene from the film 'Song of Norway'. No wonder men like Edvard Grieg and Henrik Ibsen found an everlasting inspiration in the everchanging scenery of this far flung land of mountains high and long, winding fjords.

Making my way to the Southern edge of the town, I rested on the grassy slopes of a hill, for over two hours, deeply moved by the splendid panorama of blue sea, a multitude of islands, and mountain after mountain.

Retracing my steps to the town-centre, I found the nearest hotel, and ordered a delicious evening meal. Seldom have I enjoyed a meal in such ideal surroundings, watching the evening sun slowly sink below the jagged snowy peaks, it's reflection on the fjord like a brightly burning fire.

The night train to Oslo was waiting at the now busy station, and as the train slowly left the quiet town, resting as asleep in the gathering dusk, I had a strong feeling of sadness to leave so much beauty behind.

The train entered the Romsdal valley, leaving the calm waters of the Isfjord behind, the surface of the sea glittered like a million tiny bright diamonds under a bright full moon.

The train soon passed the part of the valley which was immediately below the lofty Trolltindene peaks, the vertical walls of the Trollstigsvegan were still in shadow, and the high peaks threw long shadows across the sleeping farmsteads and sleepy meadows. Peace, perfect Peace, aptly described the rural landscape, so typical of everywhere one travels in Norway.

Slowly the train continued on it's way climbing higher and higher, past rushing mountain streams, dark pine forests, and steep mountain slopes. A new day was dawning on this blessed land which had inspired poets, painters, humanitarians, and idealists so strongly.

I have seen a moonlit night over Dartmoor, the ruins of the Ruhr, the Kremlin in Moscow, a castle in Poland, each has, in it's turn given me happiness, hope and faith.

To quote Shakespeare in 'As you like it'

> And this our life exempt from public haunt,
> Finds tongues in trees, books in the running brooks
> Sermons in stones, and good in everything
> I would not change it.

How grateful I was to have been able to visit the Romsdal and the peaceful town of Andalsnes, and to have experienced so much on that train journey from the high mountains to the fjords.

The author at Vatnahalsen on the scenic Flam Railway.

LEAVING FLÅM FOR THE SCENIC FJORD CRUISE TO GUDVANGEN.

HAMAR STATION: NORWAY'S FINE RAILWAY MUSEUM IS A SHORT WALK FROM HERE.

THE TRAIN FROM ANDALSNES PASSING THE MIGHTY TROLLTINDENE.

KJOSFOSSEN, ONE OF THE SPECTACLES OF THE FLÅM RAILWAY.

THE NORDLANDS RAILWAY.

After enjoying a hearty breakfast at Trondheim's youth hostel, and saying goodbye to my hosts, Rolf and Inger Kvam, I set off for the station, about a 15 minute's walk away. I felt so grateful for their hospitality and warm friendship which had grown over the years. It was such a free and friendly hostel, there were a few rules and regulations, but both the hosts and the majority of the guests made the atmosphere always congenial and relaxed.

Ahead was a day's journey of 450 miles on the Nordlands Railway, a journey so spectacular and exhilarating that I shall never forget it. This line had been built at tremendous effort and cost, and in 1962 it was at last completed as far as Bodo.

As the train left the station, it followed the coast very closely for many miles, and the large, prosperous farmlands, the green meadows and waving fields of ripening barley, reminded me so much of the South Wales. Trondheim is a mere 200 miles South of the Arctic Circle, and yet apple and pear trees, beech, sycamores, and lilacs grow in profusion, thanks to the warming influence of the Gulf Stream.

Levanger was the first stop after Trondheim a busy town of about 14,000 inhabitants, and not far away was Steinkjaer the softness of the landscape rapidly changed, the train left the fertile coastal belt, and the farms became scattered, with huge forests of pine, fir and spruce. The Swedish frontier was quite near and the mountains still had traces of snow on their higher slopes.

At Lake Snasvatn the Namdal valley was entered, this region is a paradise for those who love wild life and the peace and solitude of unspoilt nature. Just North of Majvatn the provice of Nordland began and this has a very sparse population, short Summers, vast tracts of forests, swamplands, and high mountains.

Along the Vefsna valley the single track crossed many bridges as it followed the valley of the River Vefsna, the high trees grew quite close to the Railway line, it was as if civilisation was a thousand miles away. At Mosjoen a lengthy halt was made, and at the small cafe, which had an atmosphere of the untamed backwoods, I enjoyed some fresh coffee and home made cake which simply melted in my mouth.

Mosjoen has a large factory processing aluminium, with the help of abundant hydro-electric power.

The high mountains, with still patches of snow on their steep slopes, almost devoid of vegetation, gave one the lasting impression of the struggle between man and nature at these high latitudes.

Mo i Rana was the next town, it had made very rapid development during the last few years. It's extensive iron and steel works were established in 1955, and most of the town's 27,000 inhabitants depend almost entirely on this industry. Most of the hydro-electric power comes from the nearby mountains, and coal, mined in Spitsbergen, is shipped during the Summer months.

Most of the houses are only a few years old, many others in the state of construction, the streets are mainly unpaved, so the town has something of the pioneer spirit.

Immediately after leaving Mo i Rana the entrance to the rugged and winding Dunderland was entered, and there was very little sign of human habitation as the train slowly and surely ascended up the valley side, closely following the swiftly flowing River Rana. The lower slopes of the mountains were covered with dense forests of dark green firs, they looked almost like ghosts in the pockets of swirling mist which was hanging over the valley. No wonder the Norwegians had fables about 'Trolls', or mountain gnomes, so vividly portrayed in the music of Edvard Grieg.

As the train reached the higher reaches of the Dunderland Valley the forest slowly became less prominent, until only stunted trees grew on the foothills of the Saltfjell mountain plateau. During the occupation of the Germans forced labour was used to extend the line, and some of the Russian and Yugoslav prisoners did not survive the privations of extremely hard work under Arctic conditions.

Near the track were several piles of stones, here the Lapps formerly worshipped and made sacrifices to their gods. As the Arctic Circle was reached, the train moved very slowly, so that we could see the high column of stones which marked its precise location.

There was a strange grandeur and fascination with the magnificent panorama of the wild spaces of windswept mountains and remote and deserted valleys. The immense and seemingly endless ranges of mountains which stretched as far as the eye could descern had a lasting impression. The high mountain peaks and steep rocky slopes took on everchanging colours and shadows as the clouds swept swiftly across the bright blue sky, like stately ships on the high seas.

Nowhere could a single trace of habitation be seen, and I had a strong feeling of joyous exhiliration.

A delightful hostess from Trondheim, called Vera, was on the train and each of us received a certificate which stated that we had passed the Artic Circle by train. As we approached the Lonsdal valley, it was pleasing to see a stunted pine tree here and there, and numerous dwarf birches. To the right was the moraine valley of the Junkerdalsaura, and in this extremely remote wilderness can be found plants which date back to the Ice Age, and only in Spitsbergen can be found similar species.

At Rognan, a station on the Saltdal Fjord, it was like being in a different world, with fields of new mown hay, and hardy crops of oats and barley. I had the opportunity to take a good look at the neat farm buildings, painted in bright colours, rustic wooden fences, and tidy stacks of sawn timber.

Fauske was a very important stop, for from here the road to the North and the route to Bodo and it's nearby mountains and islands meet. This was the last stretch of the journey, and to the South stretched the extensive range of the Borvasstindene mountains, their peaks looked just like icing on the Christmas cake, as the rays of the evening sun were reflected on the dazzling snow.

Between Bodo and the hinterland, where the Saltdal and Skerstad fjords meet, is the Saltstraumen strait, and 4 times daily 655 cubic meters of water rush through these narrow straits.

This journey of 13 hours to Bodo had a rather exhausting effect on me. and I felt almost tired out as I walked along the tidy streets and breathed in deeply the chilly air which came straight from the sea. How modern and progressive the town looked, in the last few years great progress has been made, the well planned station, modern buildings and a civic-centre which reminded me so much of the Finnish architecture, progressive and imaginative.

Bodo is a thriving fishing port, and important rail, road and air centre, being close to the Lofoten Islands and the fishing grounds.

That night of eternal light and almost continuous sunshine made sleep almost impossible, and now and then a heavy lorry would rumble slowly by, shaking the timber structure of the small guest-house where I had found accommodation. I rose early the following morning, the sea was calm under a deep blue sky, and fishing smacks chugged past, it would have made a perfect setting for a painter with the sea in his veins.

There is no railway from Fauske to Narvik, although there is a very busy station at Narvik which connects the thriving port to the huge iron ore deposits of Kiruna in the Arctic North of Sweden. So one can go by plane, boat, or bus, and I chose the latter, although I must say, how wonderful it would have been to have gone by train the whole way.

At Fauske I left the train, and waited patiently for the bus to Narvik, it was quite cold and rather damp, everyone complained of the unusually poor Summer, generally it is much warmer, and temperatures over 80 degrees fahrenheit are quite usual for short periods of time during June and July, even here it can be warmer than Italy and France at the same time.

The bus soon filled the farming families and local inhabitants and I was amazed at the amount of luggage of all shapes and sizes, it was just like an Arctic expedition, closely packed at the rear of the bus. I noticed that some of the occupants were rather short and stocky, there were probably of Lapp descent, their hair was much darker than most of the Norwegians, who, just as the Swedes, are tall and fair. The Norwegians and Swedes are the tallest nations in Europe, and they are also fortunate in that they have the highest longevity.

Passing the lower stretches of land bordering the Fauske marshes, rich in bird life, and on reaching the Sorfolla fjord, I took a ferry from Sommersett Bonasjoen. Formerly the ferry sailed from Rosvik, a trading centre founded over 200 years ago.

What a wonderful journey it was, as the bus followed the narrow winding road, flanked by thickets of birch and oddly spaced pines, with a multitude of small lakes and sparkling streams. Climbing up a very steep mountain pass at Tennvatn we were rewarded with a splendid view of seven lakes. We passed the village of Krakmo, Knut Hansum, the poet and writer lived on a farm here, and wrote his best known books, 'Segelfoss Town' and 'Growth of the Soil'.

Slowly the bus descended along the sandy road, which actually passed over the open granite outcrops without any surfacing, and suddenly I caught a panoramic view of the Lofoten islands, on the opposite side of the Vestfjord. The distance was quite great, but the atmosphere was so clear that the grandeur of the scene was even more impressive. The chain of peaks on the islands were topped by snow which were shining brightly in the clear and blue skies.

Another ferry took many passengers from Bognes to Skarberget and the surrounding mountains sloped almost vertically down into the placid waters. Stetind, rising steeply on all sides, is renown as being the finest natural obelisk in the World. Norway's narrowest point, at the head of the Tysfjord, is only 5 miles from the Swedish frontier.

The journey between the Eford and Tysfjord was at times very desolate, for here rushing water and extremes of frost had polished the mountain surfaces completely bare in places. In the narrow valleys nearer the coast the contrast was very marked, with farms and meadows, sheep and cows, and fine specimens of pine and birches.

Two more ferries were used by the heavily laden buses, and it was not long before the outskirts of Narvik were reached. Although it was late July, the lilacs and flowering shrubs were only just in bloom, for the Summer had arrived far later than usual.

I climbed the steep hill to the youth hostel, but it was full to capacity, but I was able to see much of this rather strange town, well North of the Arctic Circle.

The station staff were most helpful in finding me a room for the night at the home of a kindly old lady who lived only 3 minutes walk from the busy station. She also gave me a light supper, and flatly refused any payment.

Amongst many magazines in the small bedroom, I noticed one which vividly portrayed the life of Albert Schweitzer. It was in 1952 when he came to Oslo, to receive the Nobel Peace Prize for his devoted work in the service of humanity. The freedom-loving citizens of Oslo gave him a very moving and enthusiastic reception, and the article on this Idealist

31

and great humanitarian had a strong influence on me. In this materialistic World of modern stress and strain his aspirations and beliefs can help all mankind, regardless of race, religion, or nationality.

THE OFOTEN LINE.

Early in the morning I caught the express train which travels the whole distance from Narvik to Stockholm, the ' Venice of the North' 950 miles away (1,500 kilometers) in about 24 hours.

This railway from Narvik to Riksgrensen, on the Swedish frontier, is only 26 miles long. It is renowned not only for the part it plays in giving Swedish iron-ore access to the sea, but also for it's scenic line of a multitiude of greatly varied views. For many years this was the World's most Northerly line, and even today it is the most Northerly electrified line. And the modern C.T.C. system signalling (remote control) makes it possible to run more trains along this line than any other of Norway's single track lines. By using unattended passing loops the line gives both speed, efficiency, and safety.

The Ofoten Line is unique in that it carries roughly half the total quantity of freight of the whole Norwegian State Railways. By mutual help, both Norway and Sweden benefit by the transport of high grade Swedish iron-ore and passengers in both directions. And few journeys of 45 minutes can offer such beauty, contrast, and variation, from the wild, windswept mountain slopes, to the green and sheltered fjord pastures and their prolific woodlands.

In 1885 work commenced under the guidance of a British company for the construction of railways from the mines of Kiruna, eastwards to Lulea, on the Gulf of Bothnia, and westwards to the port of Narvik. A swedish company, Luossavaara-Kirunavaara Aktiebolaget (LKAB) was given mining rights, and this lighted the spark of initiative in the Swedish and Norwegian governments. The Norwegian State Railways recommenced work on the Ofoten Line in 1898 and 4 years later, in 1902 the line was completed. The LKAB had already built sidings, iron ore dumps, and quays, so ships were able to load their valuable cargoes at once.

Leaving the harbour, the line followed the southern side of the Rombak fjord, before making the longer and steeper climb up into the mountains. Here are several tunnels, many cuttings, and high bridges offering one sublime vista after another. At Straumes station, 6.5 miles from Narvik, is the last farm and hillside village, but further up there are no habitations, apart from the stations and linesmen's dwellings. At Rombak, only 12.5 miles from Narvik, the high mountain section commences.

Between Rombak and Katterat the line reaches an altitude of 1,150ft. and from Matterat it continues through precipieous terrain through the narrow Norddalen which is crossed by a 590 ft. long bridge, Norddalsbrua, 130 ft. above the valley bottom. From here I had a splendid view of the Rombaksbotn region, and the trees became stunted as we passed the last Norwegian station at Bjornfjell, 1,700 ft. above sea level. During the long Winter skiers flock to the neighbouring mountains, and each year about 140,000 passengers cross the border, which is rather remarkable, being well above the Arctic Circle, and remote from most of the large cities of Europe.

EXPRESS TRAIN THROUGH SWEDISH LAPLAND TO NORTHERN FINLAND.

A wonderful feeling of exhiliration rose in my heart and soul as the powerful train crossed the frontier into Swedish Lapland and came to a gentle halt at Vassijaure. At this frontier station I noticed a few window boxes at the home of the station-master, they looked so bright and cheerful, he must have been a great lover of nature and simplicity.

The land was very stony and poor, yet dwarf birches grew on patches of soil amongst the still unmelted snow, what hardy trees they are to grow at an altitude of 2,000 ft well above the Arctic Circle. And so I was in Swedish Lapland, a vast area of swamps, lakes, rivers, uninhabited mountains and forests of pine, fir, and birch trees. Lapland has great extremes of temperature, long cold Winters, and heat waves in the short but intensive Summer when the sun can shine 24 hours non-stop. Autumn comes quite rapidly, in September, in a few days the whole landscape turns into a blaze of colour too remarkable to describe before the first frost takes the leaves from the trees in one hectic rush.

Spring comes like one rapid explosion, for once the snow melts under
the rays of the brilliant sun, plant life grows at a remarkable pace.
The Swedes have taken great effort and patience to create national
parks, which are some of the largest in Europe.

I gazed up at the high mountains, their peaks still deep in snow, mosses,
grasses, and lichens on their steep slopes, which were intersected
by a multitude of rushing streams and waterfalls. Suddenly I caught
a first glimpse of Lake Tornetrask, and to the North of this silvery
expanse of water was the mountain chain which stretches across the
frontier bordering Finland, Sweden, and Norway.

What an ideal place, I though, as the train stopped at Abisko
tourist station, and a mixed group of people, chiefly Swedes, boarded
the long train. How sunburnt they were, thanks to the clear mountain
atmosphere, one could imagine they had been to southern Europe, but
not to Lapland.

Just South of the long Southern edge of the lake, I came across a Lap
settlement, smoke was rising vertically from a log cabin and it gave one
the sense of being in a lonely region of the backwood far, far away from
civilisation, which is exactly what it was. The hardy Lapps were formerly
all Nomadic, travelling with their large flocks of reindeer from the lower
lands up to the mountains in Summer, and sometimes as far as the coast
in Norway. Some even let their herds swim across the sea to some of the
larger islands bordering the coast of Norway.

About 7,000 Lapps live in Scandinavia, and also on the Kola
peninsular, in the Soviet Union. About a quarter of the Lapps derive
their living by keeping reindeer flocks, which number some 200,000,
far more than the inhabitants in this lonely region. They are completely
racially different to the Swedes, being rather short and stocky, very
industrious, with a wonderful sense of humour which is both
spontaneous and sincere.

They even grow a few crops of potatoes, rye, and oats. And today they
have excellent chances of education, and many people are helping to
solve their problems with contact from Western civilisation. Some of
them live far from the nearest town, so it is a festive occasion when
they take the long trip for a wedding or shopping in an Arctic outpost.

The reindeer is the most important means of livelihood for the Lapp and provides him and his family clothing, milk, and meat. In the Winter the herds are rounded up into compounds for careful sorting, and at this season the Lapps enjoy festivities in their brightly coloured costumes. As they run to and fro in a most energetic and lively manner, swirling their lassoes, one is reminded of a setting in a wild-west film, and the kicking of the animals hooves raise a fine mist as the fine, dry snow is disturbed.

Wearing loosely worn jackets as an insulation against the extreme cold, bright shoes of reindeer skin, peaked caps, and ornaments sometimes of pure gold or silver, they are a gay, friendly people. Indeed many of the more 'Civilised' nations could learn much from these honest and contented Northern inhabitants.

This long journey through the Lapp wilderness was about 300 miles, and most of the land was under coniferous forests. Even North of the Arctic Circle the forest grows and matures, during the short, warm Summer which lasts about 3 months, and the long hours of sunshine which is truly amazing.

After passing the iron-ore centres of Kiruna and Gallivare, the train arrived at Boden, a busy route centre situated a few miles North of the tip of the Gulf of Bothnia. A smaller train took me to Haparanda, further East, the line to this most Easterly town in Sweden was constructed in 1911. Much of the land was low, and stretches of swamps broke up the monotony of the seemingly endless forests.

Tired but still happy, I left the quiet station at Haparanda, and walked through the seemingly deserted streets of the Arctic town, most of the local inhabitants were spending their Sunday evening at home. As I crossed the bridge spanning the wide River Tournio, which seperates Finland from Sweden, the low sun's rays were reflected on it's slowly moving waters, and I thought of all the stories this bridge could tell of the multitude of peoples and nations which had crossed in peace and war.

It was strange, once on the Finnish side of the river, the atmosphere was completely different to that in Sweden, it was certainly more Eastern and the facial appearance of the people differed too.

A packed bus took me to Kemi, a thriving seaport on the estuary of the Kemijoki river. I made my way to a big restaurant in the town-centre which was packed with teenagers and young people who were enjoying Finnish and American music. The Finnish music is rather Eastern in it's character, and the 'Joika' is stimulating and lively. How I enjoyed relaxing and drinking coffee before heading for the local youth hostel.

Kemi is a very modern town, owing to many terrible fires and war damage, for Finland has for centuries experienced hardships and poverty. On reaching the youth hostel, I was so tired that I was forced to go to bed almost immediately, waking delightfully refreshed early the following morning. I was the only Englishman, but there were several Germans, Dutchmen, and Frenchmen, they were a delightfully diverse assortment, all seemed to be enjoying their holidays to the full.

So followed the last lap of the journey to Kajanni, about 150 miles away.

As the train left the more fertile coastline bordering the Gulf of Bothnia we entered a delightful landscape of rolling hills, dense forests, and small, isolated farmsteads, with their numerous wooden outhouses for the cattle, which were grazing on meadows yellow with a rich carpet of buttercups. Indeed the setting was an ideal one for the music of Jean Sibelius. Peace, perfect Peace reigned as the train glided effortlessly through the Northern forests, blue lakes sparkled in the brilliant sunshine, swallows flew overhead, it was a setting full of harmony and one felt in complete unity with the great and wonderous universe.

By late afternoon the train arrived at Kajaani, how joyous I felt to have travelled 1,500 miles, and how good it was to be able to relax with friends 3 or 4 days. Here I stayed at the home of Finnish friends, Tellervo, her Mother, and son, Tommy. They made me very welcome, and I lost no time in having my first bath since leaving Oslo.

Kajaani has about 16,000 inhabitants and is an important centre of administration. The huge timber and wood pulp and processing factory employs some 1,500 skilled and semi- skilled workers, and is the main source of employment.

Snow lies until the end of April and returns in early October, so there are only about 5 clear growing months, and often a freak frost can play havoc with the crops. Agriculture is further hampered by the great distance from markets and the rather limited size and equipment of the farms. Less than 10% of the land is cultivated, but the forests are some of the finest in Northern Europe, and about 80% is under timber. Half the forest is under pine, the rest is divided chiefly between spruce and birch.

Here the railway developed very slowly, and it was only linked with Southern Finland at the beginning of the century.

Tellervo, Tommy and I made a bus trip to Paltaniemi, a small, unspoilt village with a very old wooden church which was built in 1726. Inside this buildings, mellow with time, were some remarkable old paintings, which clearly showed the dedication, skill and infinite patience of the workers. It often took them several years to complete their details.

The Russian Czar Alexander stayed in a barn adjoining the church, his horse carriage and sturdy wooden boat are still carefully preserved. On our journey back to Kajaani, the bus passed the local airport which was situated on land recently cleared of forest. Never have I seen such an airport with such a pioneer spirit.

The time passed all too quickly, and the long return journey through Arctic Norway and Sweden awaited and beckoned me.

 After leaving Kajanni, the first large town to be reached was Oulu, a thriving seaport with about 90,000 inhabitants. It stands at the mouth of the River Oulu, which drains a wide area of Northern Finland. The river has been harnessed by .7 power stations, the electricity is used to the production of pulp, chemical, fertiliser, and engineering products.

Oulu has Finland's most Northerly university which was opened in 1959. The town library has an unusually fine selection of books, but most of the buildings are made of concrete, as a series of devastating fire have destraoyed most of the older buildings, which were very picturesque.

By early afternoon I was once again on Swedish soil, and at Haparanda a train waited to take us to Boden, where I changed trains for the third times. The last train was almost empty and, together with the huge expanses of pine, fir, and birch forests, gave one a strange sensation of being remote from the rest of civilisation. The everyday life of work and shopping, housekeeping, and a friendly chat with the neighbours seemed a thing of the past.

At Gallivare, a mining centre on the Arctic Circle, the train stopped and I was able to enjoy a fine view of the nearby Mount Dundret. Many festivities take place here, including Sweden's most important mountain celebration, the competition for the Lapland Cup. This town also has a very old wooden church, given the appropriate name 'The Iron-Ore Church', and the funds are collected by nation wide contributions.

Near here is a large and thriving Lapp settlement, and this area is the 'Cold Pole' of Sweden, being remote from the sea, and long Winters give no respite from severe frosts. and weeks without sunshine . Northwards and Westwards sped the train, the forests were still dense, but the trees were shorter, and the pine - trees gave way to the slender silver birch and slender firs. A series of small bridges spanned many rushing streams and rivers in full spate.

After what seemed an eternity, I noticed a high mountain outcrop which sood our distinctly against the endless monotony of the forest. It was the Kirunavaara mount, near Kiruna, and it contains the World's largest underground mine, and the resources of high grade iron-ore are seldom tound elsewhere.

It is a highly valuable reserve of iron-ore, and, together with it's high quality steel end products, gives a much needed revenue for Sweden's economy. And by the time I reached the mining town of Kiruna, it was almost midnight, and dusk had set in.

How deserted the town seemed, as I walked along the wide streets flanked by high birch trees in the direction of the youth hostel. The hostel had already closed for the night, and I was told there were no vacancies.

Luckily two friendly Englishmen offered me a place in a kitchen, and the only thing left was to try to sleep on a hard wooden floor with mosquitoes continually being on the attack. But at least I had a roof over my head, and the kitchen was pleasantly warm.

The hard wooden floor seemed even harder as the night of twilight slowly, very slowly passed, and I often had to move around to relieve my stiffness. And mosquitoes kept on giving me a visit, and as fast as I swept one away, another would take it's place.

Early in the morning I was well compensated by a splendid sunrise, slowly under the first rays of the rising sun, the extreme mountain tops were a blaze of purple and red, while lower down the valleys took on various shades. In many ways it reminded me of a polar landscape similar to Greenland or Spitsbergen, and only the very bottom of the valleys had sparce vegetation of dwarf birch trees.

Yet in the valleys life was in wonderous abundance, dragonflies flew nearby, with their delicate wings brightly shining in the now radiant sunshinre, swallows glided effortlessly in the clear blue sky only broken by wisps of cloud. For here, in the far North, Mother Nature is active every single moment during the long Summer days, before the long, cold Winter quickly takes it's place.

As I walked slowly to the station, the scent of newly mown grass on the city's parks was so refreshing, and the heavy dew glistened like precious jewels in the sun's life - giving rays. How grateful I felt, and so humble, to experience such quiet joy, and only when a man becomes humble can he really appreciate the goodness and beauty of nature.

The town-hall, situated towards the top of a gently sloping hill, was a perfection of simplicity, grace, and modern beauty, in some ways it resembles the Finnish architecture, which is some of the best in the World, being both full of initiative and imagination.

At the station was a Lapp lady, about 50, who was very humourous and friendly, waiting for a train. And she had a very energetic and lively Lapp dog, which soon made a fuss of me after I fould a few biscuits from my well worn and much travelled rucksack. It ate them with great relish and I felt quite reluctant to part from this magnificent specimen of health and vitality.

A fine breakfast was being served at the station, for a moderate price one could go to the open 'smargas table'. and partake of coffee, milk, grapefruit juice, bread, eggs, and cheese, not forgetting jams, cornflakes and porridge. It was a meal fit for a king, and my spirits quickly rose as I alighted on to the waiting train, bound for my beloved Norway.

And soon I was once again on the move, speeding effortlessly amongst magnificent scenery, as the train approached the steeply sloping Western shores of Lake Tornetrask. It was very misty, with patches of chilly drizzle clinging to the tracks. Suddenly a light breeze sprung up and I was fortunate to have an uninhibited view of Lapporten, which is a clearly defined cleft in the high mountain chain. Through this pass, from time immemorial, the hardy Lapp nomads with their large herds of reindeer wandered in search of grazing grounds, on their annual migrations from East to West.

After reaching Narvik I longed to return to Southern Norway, and after going by bus to Fauske, caught the night-train to Trondheim. And as I left the train at Trondheim, it seemed like a wonderful homecoming, after travelling well over a thousand miles since leaving Kajaani through the Arctic regions.

The tiredness disappeared as if by magic as I walked amongst the rather busy streets, people intent on getting to work on time, and early morning shoppers who too were enjoying the warmth of the sunshine which brought out the bright colours of the well-kept shops and stores.

It was just like coming back to civilisation as I admired the paved streets and tidy gardens and parklands. The historical buildings are carefully preserved by the town administration, and this cathedral town still retains it's timeless atmosphere inspite of modern progress and factories, which are situated on the outskirts of the town.

Rolf, the tall, friendly warden, and his wife, Inger, had read a book I gave them before leaving 2 weeks ago, and they gave me a warm welcome, so typical of the Norwegian people, with their spontaneous friendly attitude towards tourists, especially the British, who they greatly admire.

After the long journey, with lack of daily exercise, I longed to do some useful work, so the same morning I began work in the garden, digging some rough ground, taking away loads of stones, and preparing a lawn. How happy I felt, to live and work at this friendly hostel, with a splendid view over the Trondheim fjord, the nearby Munkholmen fortress, and the mountains towering above the calm waters.
The hostel was very modern, and often over 200 tourists stayed there during the busy season.

The warden and his wife were only too pleased to take me out in their old British car, and show me some of the interesting sights of Trondheim. A Dutch girl, who had also stayed at Haraldsheim hostel in Oslo, the previous year, was very surprised to meet me there. Her brother was a specialist in ornithology, and she had spent some time with him studying bird migrations in Sweden, Poland, and Germany.

One evening we spent much of the time watching a wonderous sunset from the hostel lounge. The quiet waters of the fjord changed their colour slowly from one shade to another in the darkening twilight;

Rolf, together with his 2 sons, Peter and Gunnar, took me out walking in the forest. The crips air from the forests and hills made me feel so energetic and enthusiastic. This was living in it's finer and truer sense, enjoying abundant health and rejoicing in the grandeur of the surroundings.

I recollected part of the Norwegian National Anthem — 'And, when night in falling, brings as dreams to Earth'.

The happy days of my brief stay in Trondheim came rather abruptly to an end, and the time came to say farewell to my kindly hosts before returning to Oslo. I felt rather sad as I walked along the quiet streets towards the station. As I crossed over the old wooden bridge, I found time to gaze over the waters of the winding River Nidda, which shone gently in the early morning sunshine.Swallows glided effortlessly over-head, it was a true token of a fond farewell and an even happier return to my beloved Trondheim.

NIGHT EXPRESS TO STOCKHOLM — VENICE OF THE NORTH.

Several eventful years had passed since I was in Stockholm, where I once worked a few months as a gardener. It would be highly interesting to know how much change and progress had been made since those carefree days, when traffic was much lighter and high blocks of flats were less conspicuous.

As the train passed through Eastern Norway, the track followed the course of the slowly flowing River Glomma, which was very wide. This is the widest river in Norway, and also the longest, 380 miles, and it has a huge potential for both hydro-electric power and timber floating. It was almost dark, but sometimes a shaft of light was reflected on the waters, and I could see the outlines of drifting logs.

Soon sleep overcame me, and when I awoke, I was already in Sweden.

What an enchanted night it was, the slender pine and fir trees stood outlined against the cold, clear sky, and the stars twinkled brightly in the vast firmanent above, there must have been thousands of them, the atmosphere was so clear.

This was the province of Varmland, large and sparsely inhabited, with an unusual variety of natural beauty, and the people are extremely hospitable and also industrious and enterprising.

Slowly the stars faded from the sky as the first signs of dawn became visible on the Eastern horizon. I gazed at the immense solitude of lakes, forests, and swampland, abundant in wild-life and birds. Through the dead traces of the previous years vegetation were the fresh green shoots of early Spring. Willow and birch saplings were mirrowed in the quiet waters and the amber hue of the morning sky was reflected on a scale which could be described as being truly festive.

At Karlstad, the provincal capital, a lengthy halt was made. What a beautify setting this picturesque town has, being situated on the shores of Sweden's largest lake, Lake Vaner, and at the mouth of the Klara Alv River. Millions of logs float down this river for the paper and pulp mills.

All true garden lovers should visit the Rottneros mansion, situated to the North, with it's fine sculptures and fascinating gardens Selma Lagerlof, the famous Swedish writer lived here, and found many an inspiration from the stillness of the forest, the wideness of the skies, and the splendour of the Lake Fryken which came to the very slopes of the mansions's grounds.

In this splendid province of water and sky, forest and hill, one is completely surrounded by unspoilt beauty wherever one goes. The train slowly departed from the now almost empty station, still in the midst of slumber, and a poem I had written came to my mind.

VARMLAND – A SWEDISH PARADISE.

Clouds float like ships across the sky so blue
Birches green sway gently int he breeze
Here are woods and valleys
Far from the city's noise and hue
Where one finds Peace and Joy

42

Onwards the train sped towards the East, here the forests were slightly less dense, giving way to large farming areas, interspersed with a delightful blending of lakes and wooded hills. It reminded me so much of the North European Plains, which continue from German to Poland and the Sovier Union. The fields were already a bright, fresh green, with the shoots of oats, wheat, and barley.

Rapidly growing towns like Vasteras and Enkoping were passed, and soon we were amonst the suburbs of Stockholm. It was so beautiful, passing over several bridges, and still plenty of open spaces and parks.

The train pulled in to Stockholm's Central Station, and I was amazed how modern and well - planned it was, nowhere have I seen such a station in Europe, it was also bright and artistic.

A number of shops and kiosks were doing a busy trade, supplying bread, milk, chocolates, and even shirts and ties. The snack bars and banks were already open.

Leaving the station, everything seemed to have changed, many of the older buildings had been replaced by high blocks of flats, and wide streets giving easy access to the shopping centres. Had it not been for the nearby Lake Malar, it would have been difficult to have found my way around.

I found a small cafe at Tegelbacken, quite near the shore, and from a window-seat had a good view of the Royal Palace, the Vasa Bridge but what attracted me most was the broad expanse of Lake Malar,it's blue waters reflecting the bright sunshine, almost like a blessing sublime.

As I walked on, it seemed remarkable to notice a fisherman who was netting a few fish only a few yards from the Royal Palace. I passed the Royal Opera House, one of the oldest in Europe, which is near the Stadsholmen island, the old centre of Stockholm. This today is extremely well preserved as a historical monument of lasting greatness. A mere 5,000 domicile here, and each day a further 15,000 commute from the suburbs.

And so I came to Stockholm's down town area, just North of Strommen, this is a stretch of water around which the harbour, older buildings, and ramparts were constructed. Three quarters of the Stockholmers live in the modern suburbs, and a total of two thirds work in the City.

At Hotorgs city, the old houses have vanished, and in their place has been constructed a splendid shopping street which is just for pedestrians only. And, equally important, the Stockholmers look forward without forgetting their historical past. Much effort has been exerted to preserve the older buildings and the beautiful views of this modern, clean, and progressive town.

Sweden was fortunate enough to look ahead with the traffic problem in their larger towns. Even in 1940, when the population was only 800,000 the initiative was taken to build the first subways. In 1945 work was in full progress, and by 1957 the first subways had 25 miles of track and 47 stations. This network connects the Western and Southern suburbs of the city with it's centre.

In addition, a second subway system joins the South Western suburbs with the centre, and is being expanded to reach the North - Eastern regions. Vast sums are being invested to improve the town's roads, the Stockholm citizens were wise enough to widen streets, and to turn some into pedestrian walks.

As the long, warm evening of the Summer slowly descended on this Northern Venice, I lost no time exploring some of the town centre. On the water front I found the perfect setting of water, sky, and land, to be an eternal symbol of beauty, space, and imagination which is peculiar to Stockholm, and, to a less extent Helsinki.

Looking across the wide stretch of Lake Malar, the numerous lights from a multitude of buildings, large and small, were reflected on it's waters, a soft amber from the bright sky of the setting sun.

So followed a rather hurried return to the Central Station, a hasty meal, and rapid rush to catch the awaiting train. In no time the warmth of the bright and clean compartment brought relaxation to my tired muscles and active mind, and in no time I was completely lost in a blissful sleep.

It was farewell to the Venice of the North and another Happy Return to Norway the Sublime.

ACROSS NORTHERN SWEDEN TO MY BELOVED TRONDHEIM.

One beautiful warm evening Oslo, when the sun was low in the Western sky, I received a long - distance telephone call from Trondheim. The warden of Trondheim Youth Hostel told me he greatly needed my help to put the hostel gardens in order. It came only just in time for the following day I had intended to travel by an early train to Gothenburg, the thriving port on the West Coast of Sweden.

Yet this change of plan proved to be a golden opportunity, and instead of travelling directly to Trondheim, I decided to first change trains after arriving in Stockholm, and then cross Northern Sweden and see something of the magnificent mountain scenery which is to be found on the Swedish -Norwegian frontier, on the high mountain chain.

As I left Stockholm in the late evening, the train did not take long to reach the fertile undulating farmlands of Uppland. From this ancient cultural centre the pagan Vikings planned their adventurous explorations. These Vikings of great courage, energy, and determination sailed great distances to hitherto unknown shores. They even sailed down the length of the River Volga, and founded the Ancient Russia.

There was a very close connection between Swedish Upland and the Anglo-Saxon kingdom of East Anglia, where the settlers practised the cults of the heathen gods before the advent of Christianity.

The Cathedral and University town of Uppsala was the first stop. It has splendid botanical gardens, and a university of high reputation of World fame, equalled only by Lund university in South Sweden. That gifted genius Von Linneaus did much to classify plant species, he made scientific expeditions to many lands, and his works today are still of useful help to many botanists. Near Uppsala are ancient burial mounds, and the Uppland Vikings made pagan sacrifices to their gods Oden, Fro, and Tor.

Onwards the train sped Northwards, into a strange and silent World, for only a few miles from Uppsala, civilisation seemed so remote, as the fields and meadows were no more, and in their place was mile after mile of seemingly endless forest. The dark forms of the firs and pines were outlined against the faint glow of the Twilight in the Western sky.

Then sleep overcame me, and when I awoke, the sun was low on the

Eastern horizon, and on either side were rolling hills so thickly forested that it was sometimes impossible to see more than a few hundred yards. Sometimes the track passed close to a remote farm, which had been literally wrested from the forest by clearing the trees and ploughing up the soil after removing the trunks and rocks and boulders. These are the men I admire, who work by their own hard efforts to earn their daily bread, not expecting an easy life, but rather doing things by one's own initiative, by patience and good-will.

The hay had been hung up to dry, suspended on wires strung between wooden posts, and the meadows were a blaze of yellow buttercups which are a delight to the eyes for all idealists who love the nature of Scandinavia.

Later in the morning the train reached Sundsvall, I was amazed at the size of this Northern town, with it's wide, straight avenues flanked by fresh green birch trees. The buildings were very modern and impressive, the older wooden houses were only to be seen on the town's outskirts. Sundsvall is the most important port in the whole of Northern Sweden for the export of timber, wood pulp, and many other important wood products to a multitude of lands, In the Winter the port is ice-bound for 3 or 4 months, and the citizens are once again in high spirits when the first ship of the Spring arrives.

After leaving Sundsvall the train headed in a Westerly direction, and amongst the huge coniferous forests, one could well imagine being in the heart of Siberia. The train followed very closely the course of the River Ljungan, a huge, wide river which flowed at a very slow pace.

Past Ange the land was slightly higher, and I saw many large lakes and rushing waterfalls before reaching Ostersund, where I was able to enjoy a hearty breakfast. Ostersund is beautifully located on Lake Froson, and is also exactly situated in the centre of Sweden. And yet it is as far away from Malmo, in the South of Sweden, as London is from the South of France.

From Ostersund there is a magnificent view towards the distant mountains of Jamtland, close to the Norwegian frontier. The Swedish poet and writer Peterson Birger found peace of mind and inspiration while living near Ostersund.

The line slowly climbed towards the mountains, and I could see range after range of high mountains towards the Western horizon, their jagged peaks gleaming white in all their rugged splendour. How I liked the mountain resort of Are, with it's green valleys neasling at the foot of the Areskutan mountain. Are is perhaps the most popular skiing resort throughout the length and breadth of Sweden.

As the altitude increased the trees became stunted, with swamps and thickets of dwarf birches and firs. Storlien, altitude nearly 2,000 ft (592 meters) 430 miles from Stockholm (709 kilometers)was the last frontier station before reaching that wonderful Land of the Midnight Sun, Norway.

There was a most remarkable change of the mountain landscape, for the mountains on the Norwegian side are much steeper. The descent was far more rapid, and for long stretches the brakes were applied. And what a scenic panorama it was, as the track curved round the steep mountains in wide arcs of a circle, the splendour of the views were changing every few minutes. High forests grew on the steep slopes, for Trondelag has some of the finest forests in the whole of Norway. On the lower ground were glimpses of the rushing River Stjorsdal and the temperature rose to the lower eighties, making me perspire profusely.

We passed the small station by the famous name of Hell, how funny it sounded as the ticket collector announced,half smiling,'Attention please, next stop Hell'. How good it was to see the blue expanse of the Trondheim fjord, with many people, especially children, basking in the sun on the small beaches, or taking a trip in their colourful sailing boats.

A journey of nearly 1,000 miles had come to an end since leaving Oslo, and it was good to know I could soon relax and do some useful garden-work. Rolf, the kindly warden, and his friendly, hard-working wife, Inger, made me feel so welcome. As I enjoyed a delicious meal we discussed plans for the garden, and later their sons cam home from school, Peter and Gunnar were intent on asking me questions about my travels, Peter, the older son could already speak fluent English.

The Trondheim Youth Hostel was high up on a hill overlooking the scenic Trondheim Fjord, and the land was very stony with grass and thick weeds, so we deicded to buy a few hundred shrubs to improve the garden. Rolf drove me out to a market garden outside the town and the manager, Lars, was a typical Norwegian, slim and blond, with happy keen, blue eyes. He had worked a year in America, and was very fond of English people.

47

Soon I was busy planting the shrubs, chiefly contoneaster and berberis, which can withstand extreme cold, and thrive well above the Artic Circle. Suddenly a heat wave enveloped Norway, it went well into the eighties, but I quite enjoyed the blazing sunshine.

A Norwegian family I met at the hostel in Gothenburg lived quite near the hostel, just below the hill, so one evening I joined Erling and Aslaug for a meal at their home. Erling was extremely friendly and very international-minded and tolerant, being an active member of the Esperanto Society. When I left their home at about 11p.m. the sun was slowly sinking below the mountains fringing the Trondheim Fjord, and the whole sky was a blaze of crimson, and even at midnight the purple glow of twilight still was present.

And when I arrived at the hostel, they invited me for a midnight tour of Trondheim. We saw the Stiftsgarden, this is the largest wooden building in Northern Europe, and has been a royal residence since the crowning of King Haakon VII in 1906. It is about 200 years old and like many other old buildings, chiefly of wooden construction, was built by local and foreign craftsmen. After a brief walk in the woods above the town, we drove along the road called 'Fridjof Nansen' in lasting tribute to a fine Norwegian idealist. The ships in the harbour were at anchor on a sea so blue, and the sky was a bright as day. So, passing the old fortress of Kristiansen, we returned, happy and tired to a much wanted sleep.

Trondheim has a delightful unspoilt atmosphere of unhurried peace and calm, the citizens work well, but they know how to relax, and what they cannot do today, they proceed with the following one. I often spent a pleasant hour at one of the bookshops near Var Frue Church, and the shopkeepers were always so patient and understanding.

For every Englishman with feeling and sentiment, love of beauty and unspoilt charm, Trondheim and it's hospitable people make a journey to Norway something of lasting interest and enjoyment.

NORTHWARD BOUND TO ARCTIC SWEDEN AND FINNISH LAPLAND.

After finishing my work for the season, I decided to make a journey from Oslo to Northern Sweden and Finnish Lapland, a very strenuous journey of about a thousand miles. Leaving Oslo early in the morning on the Stockholm express, I reached Kil in the province of Warmland, and changed trains in order to save time by not passing through Stockholm. The province of Dalarna was thickly forested and sparsely populated, and towns were small and few. The train stopped at Sandviken, famous for it's high grade steel products, especially saws and tools, which are exported all over the world.

Mineral deposits give rise to small mining and factory settlements, and small towns such as Falun, Borlange, and Ludvika play an important role in the efficient Swedish economy, chiefly in the production of machinery, which is extremely strong and durable.

It was already evening by the time I reached Gavle, a very large port with extensive wharves and many factories. With it's 70,000 inhabitants, it is about the same size as Sundsvall, and these two towns are the two most important towns in Northern Sweden. One could sense the feeling of remoteness rather peculier to Northern Sweden, so different to Denmark and the West Coast of Sweden, which have fairly mild Winters.

I felt quite excited as I alighted on the express train which travels from the busy heart of Central Stockholm across vast tracts of Northern Sweden and Lapland to Narvik, a distance of about 950 miles (approx. 1,540 kilometers), in under 24 hours. There are several long bridges on this line, as the track bridges many of the long rivers which flow chiefly in a Southeasterly direction towards the Gulf of Bothnia.

The railway was built about 25 to 60 miles inland to develop new territory and avoid the wide mouths of the rivers.

The line is single track and heavily graded, and forms an important route for passenger and freight traffic, especially in the Winter, since neither the bulk nor the value weight ratio favour air transport.

Gavle is the county town and regional centre for Southern Norrland and Northern Uppland, and has metal, textile, and pottery industries, as well as sawmills, pulp and paper works. The group of towns along the Dal river which include Sandvika, Hofors and Gavle is one of the few zones of population growth in Norrland.

By the time the train reached Bollnas, a small industrial town and route centre it was already dark, and already people near the platform were wearing thick winter coats.

The train was delightfully warm, and I even perspired gently and it made me realise what modern progress has achieved, and it seemed difficult to realise that outside were the huge coniferous forests of Sub-Artic Sweden. I managed to sleep a few hours, and caught a glimpse of Sundsvall, situated at the mouth of the Ljungan and Indal river mouths. I was amazed to learn later that all the wood processing plants are under the control of one firm. Swedish Cellulose, which owns 430,000ha/1,660 sq. miles of forest, about the size of Lancashire.

Sleep once again overpowered me, and, when I awoke it was just early dawn, which was breaking gently over the grey hills. It was impossible to see very far, owing to the dense forest, but when the train passed over a bridge or cutting, some of the views were quite spectacular. Throught the night I had traversed several hundred miles of lonely forest, sometimes it was over a hundred miles between two towns.

After passing the villages of Bastutrask and Alvsbyn, it was heartening to glimpse the outskirts of Boden through a clearing in the forest. There was already a crisp Autumn tang in the atmosphere as I walked at ease along the wide streets of Boden, which were often flanked by graceful birch trees, now full of light and splendour in their Autumn colour. The town was beautiful, and it's gardens spacious and well planned and yet I missed Norway with it's rather old fashioned towns of quiet atmosphere, with brightly painted cottages on the hillsides behind the towns.

In the afternoon I caught a local bus to the port, Lulea, where some friends, Dan and Madelaine lived. Dan had just come home from work and was only too pleased to show me some of the spectacular point of interest around the town. First we drove to the western perimiter of the town, and climbed to the summit of a high hill which was being turned into a ski-jump. The sun was setting far to the west, and below me stretched a vast expanse of forest, a dark green which merged into the far distant hills.

Of great interest was the old wooden church, which was once used by countrymen and farmers who came a very long way to attend services. To make their stay more enjoyable, several hundred small cottages had been built. closely huddled together, to give them shelter for the night. The horses were also given food, shelter, and attention. It was surprising to see a place of such cultural importance so far North were the population was sparse.

Lulea, the county town of Norrbotten, is also the Southern terminus of the iron-ore railway, and about 5 million tons of iron-ore are shipped each year. The town's iron and steel works use about 700,000 tons of iron-ore to produce 600,000 tons of steel. Pressed steel parts are manufactured for the motor assembly plant at Sodertalje, near Stockholm. Dan showed me round the docks, which were very extensive and modern, so typical of the Sweden of today.

On our return to their home, I had the pleasure of joining Dan and Madelaine to a delightfully prepared supper. of fish, potatoes, vegetables, and hard bread, seldom have I enjoyed such a delicious meal. We finished with tea and home made cakes by a blazing log fire with a fragrant scent from the smoldering pine-logs.

What a divine way to finish a highly eventful and strenuous day, before sleeping soundly for many hours.

The parents of Madelaine were old friends of mine who I had known for many years while working in Gothenburg., so we had many happy memories and much to talk about. Dan worked for a road haulage firm, but even though the wages and working conditions were very promising he longed to live in Southern Sweden, where the Winters were much shorter. I felt indeed more than grateful as I left them at the station.

After changing trains at Boden, I continued on my journey to Haparanda through huge forests and lonely swampland which seemed endless. Many of the villages, such as Lapp trask had typical Lapp names, for a high percentage of the natives are of Lapp origin.

Crossing the wide Tornetrask river, I was once again in Tornio, the sun shone warm and brightly, and it was it was difficult to believe one was only a short distance from the Arctic Circle, the fertile soil and short but warm Summers made it possible to grow some of the hardy crops, such as barley and rye.

Kemi was the next stop, a very busy but small industrial town specialising in the manufacture and export of wood products. Finland has a great demand for her hydro-electric plants, both for factory and home consumption, and the rivers in the North, such as the Kemi and Oulu are valuable sources of supply.

I boarded the bus to Rovaniemi, my final destination and capital of Finnish Lapland. Arctic Finland covers a huge area, but there are only 45,000 inhabitants outside the towns of Kemijarvi and Rovaniemi. Snow covers the ground from late October until the middle of May, so the forest growth is less than a third compared with the far South of Finland.

The rather narrow and winding road was paved for a few miles, and followed closely the course of the large Kemijoki river. The land was amazingly well cultivated and fairly level. Farming families and lumbermen, who looked as hard and strong as the wood they felled, carried on rather light hearted conversation as the rather overloaded bus rattled along the uneven road surface, with an occasional pothole to make us all lurch forward in a most unexpected manner.

A single track railway ran almost parallel with the road, and I noticed one or two power stations. And there was a very rapid change in the landscape, the large farmsteads were less numerous, instead forests stretched as far as the eye could see. To the East were high hills rising abruptly from the plateaux, their higher slopes were only covered with clumps of dwarf mountain birches.

Most of the passengers had alighted, and as the almost empty bus sped onwards in the rapidly descending dusk, a strange feeling of melancholy and complete isolation seemed to pervade the very atmosphere. The noise of the engine droned in my tired ears, while outside the beams from the headlamps lit up the ragged outlines of the slender spruce trees. Time stood still, on this seemingly endless Arctic journey.

Suddenly, as the bus swerved round a sharp bend, I caught my first glimpse of Rovaniemi. In the far distance were the lights of this strange Northern town, and as the bus neared it's destination, the lights were reflected on the waters of the River Kemi.

The bus came to a grinding halt at the terminal, brightly lit below a dark sky, overcast with heavy low clouds.

The bus station was very busy, buses arriving and departing, and the waiting room and large restaurant had an atmosphere of loud music, local gossip, a strong aroma of good, homely cooking, fresh coffee, and the thick haze of tobacco smoke. It reminded me so much of a wild-west film.

Apart from being a centre of administration for Arctic Finland, Rovaniemi is an important tourist centre, and there are frequent bus services to all the Northern settlements. The railway line has been laid to a junction with the Soviet Leningrad-Murmansk line. There are Winter tourist centres towards the North, especially in the Munio valley, where Finnish territory extends into the more mountainous terrain of Western Scandinavia. The village of Sodankyla has a very useful centre which specialises in forestry research under Arctic conditions. Often several buildings of administration are closely linked together, as they can be supplied by one centre of heating, which is a great economy in extremly cold conditions.

I caught a bus to the youth hostel, and as the bus slowly lumbered through the town, I found time to ponder. The town was certainly modern, with an excellent library, modern station, office blocks and housing estates. Yet it still retained a strong pioneer spirit, surrounded by vast tracks of forests, lonely spaces, and extreme and rapid temperature changes. Anyone who lived here would need plenty of books and indoor hobbies to keep one occupied during the long winter months.

From the bus stop to the youth hostel it was a good ten minutes walk along a quiet road, the air was mild and damp, and I often found myself stepping into puddles. The warden and his wife made me welcome, but I was too tired to hold much conversation, so I said goodnight.

When I awoke the sun was shining through the pine and birch trees on to the grassy slopes and moss covered rocks and stones. And much to my surprise two Englishmen asked me to join them for breakfast, I was rather short of time, and just had a sandwich and quick cup of coffee.

As I waited for the local bus, a small boy appeared, and in his hand was a piece of paper, written in English, which stated 'I am a boy scout are you a scout too?' Unfortunately a bus came round the corner and I was obliged to wave goodbye to this kindly boy and friendly dog. It was rather a moving meeting, and I felt both sad and reluctant to leave them so quickly.

The bus passed a large school, I noticed many children playing in the courtyard, judging by their laughter and noise, they seemed a very happy lot. How good it would be to give them a lesson in English, I thought, and this sense of duty compelled me to alight at the next stop, and walk along to the community school.

A lady teacher, Mrs. Kuivalainen, introduced me to her class, and I thoroughly enjoyed speaking to the children, who were unusually attentive. One boy stated his favourite sport was Bingo. Truly, human-nature is the same the world over.

It seemed so strange, and yet so worthwhile, being able to talk to some friendly, joyous children who lived in the Arctic, and very few had ever seen an Englishman before. We can learn much from children, their friend-ship is so spontaneous, and they enjoy asking questions and are usually willing to learn. A journey is always twice as rewarding if we make good friendships en route or at our destination.

The return journey was rather rapid and uneventful, but I noticed how much more advanced the Autumn had progressed compared with Southern Sweden and Norway. Already the air had become much colder, and an occasional flurry of wind sent the rich brown and bright amber leaves fluttering gently to the ground. I changed trains at Boden, after catching trains at Kemi and Haparanda.

It was about 800 miles by train from Boden to Stockholm, and I was able to make friends with an elderly lady who I helped with her luggage. The train was only about a third full, and yet it was warm and comfortable, compared with the chilly air outside, how thankful I felt.

Soon night descended on the Northern forests and lakes, on and on sped the train through the inky darkness, seldom could a light be seen in this region of sparce population and remoteness of industrial towns. Once the train stopped at a lonely siding, to allow an express train going in the opposite direction, to pass. I looked out, and the stars shone brightly in a clear, cold sky. The trees had grown so rapidly during the short Summer that their branches were brushing against the coaches.

When I awoke it was quite light, it was about 80 miles South of Sundsvall, the forests were truly remarkable, fine trees of pine and spruce a sight to make any lover of trees rejoice deep down in his heart. Now and then I caught a brief glimpse of farms,they possessed extensive clearings for crops and pasture for their sturdy cattle.

In the province of Halsingland, I saw the first apply tree, this was a sure sign that the climate was more suitable for human habitation, and some of the forest trees were indeed majestic giants, full of strength and dignity.

Arriving at Gavle, it was a homecoming to civilisation, and the size of the busy port compared differently to the smaller settlements of the Northern territory. Even from the window of my compartment I could see the outlines of the masts and rigging of cargo ships in the harbour. The traffic on the streets was already heavy, people were intent on reaching their places of employment. The half empty train was, in the passing of a few minutes, almost full to capacity, business men and artisans were travelling to Stockholm, for in Sweden, as in Finland and Norway, most of the population lived in the South of the land.

How different the landscape became, North of Gavle the sparse population had little influence of the wild, unspoilt Nature, but further South, there were large farms and many villages and small towns. Here snow cover was only three to four months, compared to six or seven near Boden. And the timber matured three times as quickly as in the North.

It was showery and overcast in Stockholm, and the rain clouds gave the town a rather dreary atmosphere. But I felt just as happy, for in this fine metropolis there was always much to see, much to do, and much to learn. The shopping centre caught my attention, and I was able to find time to purchase a few presents and souvenirs for friends.

I visited the Public Relations department of the Swedish State Railways, and expressed my gratitude for their spontaneous help and useful information. Towards the early evening the clouds slowly dispersed from the skies, and the sight of a splendid sunset gave one a feeling of elation and inspiration.

Stockholm was revealed in all her fascination and splendour. It was just as if time stood still to portray the perfect harmony of land, water, and sky, the stately houses and slender buildings, bridges, parks and tree-lined avenues.

As I strolled through the wide lit streets, I noticed how hurredly the Stockholmers were in their desire to reach home as quickly as possible. Yet I found it impossible to hurry at such a pace, I just wanted to have the necessary time to more fully appreciate the beauty of the sunset scene. As I reached the waterfront at Tegelbacken, not far from the Royal Palace, the graceful outline of the town hall was silhouetted against the western sky, still bright with a deep crimson glow. From here I headed for the youth hostel, known as 'Af Chapman', a former old sailing schooner. The last booking had been already taken just a few minutes before I arrived, but I did not feel downhearted, for one cannot be lucky all the time. Glancing across the wide sweep of Lake Malar, a thousand city lights were reflected on it's waters, still retaining the faint glow of the Western sky.

While waiting for an old friend, Sture, I was fortunate to be able to meet, just by chance, at a hotel kiosk selling newspapers and postcards, an energetic, educated Englishman, Mr. Martin, and an Amercian lady, full of the joy of living, Jennifer Harris. They, together with other teachers, were busy administrating an Institute for Personal Development, and I found them very interesting and inspiring company.

After spending a very happy evening with Sture and his family, I took the underground railway to the modest hotel where I had booked a room. Sleep did not come easily that night, as my mind was too alert, I saw the dawn break, and heard the first twitterings of the birds, before the noise of the ever-increasing traffic became louder. Leaving the hotel, I again headed for the 'Af Chapman' youth hostel, for what better than to enjoy a breakfast 'Al fresco' with a view over the blue waters of Lake Malar. The sun shone brightly on the glittering waters of Strommen, I felt on top of the World....

A short time was taken after breakfast speaking to a kindly American negro who had studies at the same college as Martin Luther King, and I noticed how he radiated happiness and peace of mind.

It was just one long, last look at the multitude of shops before catching the express train to Gothenburg. The train was like a magic carpet, speeding across the plains of Central Sweden, the bright Autumn sun lit up the landscape in a splendour of colour, rich and mellow, as if the Mother Earth slept in sweet repose, after the sweat and toil of the hot Summer.

Sweat and toil may seem unpleasant words, but is not life an unending struggle. Yet in this struggle we gain inner strength and the power to learn to improve ourselves and gain added zest for living.

Near Falkoping and Herrljunga, where the terrian was rather higher, there was a splendid panorama towards the East, with huge tracts of forests and glistening lakes, and above was a clear blue sky with faint traces of high clouds.

Once again I was at Gothenburg station, a place that brings back many happy memories in a sentimental way. The station, with it's high beams and arches, wooden panelwork, and rather narrow main - entrance, still retains something of the old fashioned spirit, which is often sadly lacking in modern, progressive Sweden.

How many journeys I have made from Gothenburg, to Oslo in Norway, Copenhagen in Denmark, Warszawa in Poland, and Stockholm and Finland. There is something of Gothenburg station which the Swedes call 'Hemtrevlig' or 'homely' in English.

Autumn had certainly come to Gothenburg, it no longer retained the gay Summer atmosphere of the town I have grown to love, the people wore overcoats or thick leather jackets, and laughter was no longer so spontaneous as during the long, sunny days. The strong gusts of winds caught the falling leaves of the oaks, beeches, and chestnuts and sent them in a flurry across the wet streets and high pavements.

Time had passed all too quickly, the short Spring which had come in a mere few days, turning the surroundings into a pattern of bright greens. the warm Summer days when night was almost non-existent, and now the mellow Autumn, which brought a delightful freshness to the air of a sunlit September day. Soon I would experience another Autumn, home with my good Mother in England, Autumn last even longer, thanks to the mildness of the climate.

So it was a joyous farewell to the mountains and fjords forests and lakes of the Northern lands, and their friendly, hospitable people. Happy meetings, lasting friendships, delightful memories, had made my travel so full of well-rewarded happiness and fulfilment.

For is not life a great adventure which we share with our fellow men. And though full of hardships, it is made by human effort and endeavour into an undescribable, festive occasion.

THE CONSTRUCTION OF THE BERGEN RAILWAY.

Norwegian workmanship, initiative, and skill conquers high mountains.

A brilliant Norwegian, with an inborn sense of duty and foresight, Mr. H.A. Gloersen, was greatly influenced by the building of the Mount Cenis tunnel. This 8 mile (12Km.) tunnel was completed on 25th December, 1870 after 13 years of dedicated, hard-work, and formed a vital link between France and Italy.

Only half a year after this tunnel was completed, Mr. Gloersen of Bergen, wrote an article in a newspaper with the useful idea of the construction of a railway between Bergen and Kristiania. His sincerity, practical information, and determination, gave him the worthy title of 'The Father of the Bergens Railway.'

There were many lengthy discussions and debates in the Storting (Government building) which reached it's climax the 1st March, 1894. The various committees had talked over several alternatives which had been recommended and discussed. The Government had decided to build the railway through the Raundadalen valley and then across the mountains, before descending into the long and winding Hallingdal.

The greatest construction problems were the mountains and one of the strongest opponents broke into one of the meetings with a telegram that 12 to 14 meters (about 36 ft) of snow had fell on the mountains. After 4 days intensive debate the president took up the votes. With 60 against 53 votes the Stortinget gave the decision to build a railway from Voss to Taugevatn.

It was to take 15 years to complete the railway in it's entirety, and in Bergen the people were so high-spirited that they celebrated for a full three days.

BERGEN-OSLO EXPRESS TRAVERSING THE HARDANGERVIDDA, EUROPE'S LARGEST MOUNTAIN PLATEAU, NEAR FINSE.

NORWEGIAN STATE RAILWAYS

The Dovresprinten from Trondheim to Oslo halts at Otta, in Gudbrandsdalen, gateway to the Jotunheimen and Rondane mountains

AN EXPRESS FROM STOCKHOLM SPEEDS PAST STENHAMMAR'S CASTLE
NEAR FLEN IN CENTRAL SWEDEN.

SWEDISH RAILWAYS

SEPTEMBER IN LAPPLAND: A NARVIK-LULEA TRAIN AT ABISKO TURISTSTATION.

THE DIFFICULT AND DANGEROUS CONSTRUCTION.

The festivities were also mixed with doubt, for to build a railway for 100km. (60 miles) across high mountains with windswept wilds and eternal snow was a technical feat which never could succeed.
The historian Ludvig Daae was one of the sceptics, for he argued that not only the terrain was the main obstacle, but also the differences between the peoples of East and West Norway. This would turn the West into a self-governed republic, and so Norway would be divided.

When the work began on the construction of the stretch from Voss to Taugevatn in 1895, there were many times which were extremely difficult for those fine, determined workers, and it took 6 years to terminate the strenuous work.

Many of the lonely areas were completely devoid of houses or dwellings of any kind, so often the workers were compelled to live in tents and endure primitive conditions in a harsh climate of rapid temperature changes.

The food, drink, clothing and many other essentials had to be hauled by horses from the nearest mountain village.

Once the first stone huts were in position, an essential advance was achieved. The first was built at Memorge, west of Taugevatn, and it was of great help in assessing the conditions of the snow at the highest point of the proposed railway. In 1896, 2 more huts were erected, near Laghellervatn in Moldadalen, and one with Sandavatn in Finsedalen. Still a tent and sleeping sack was much in use for some of the personnel.

The work involved was both highly strenuous and dangerous, for the courageous men would have to work near a sheer precipice, or adjust themselves to the steep side of a high mountain. And to make things even worse, it was cold and depressing, with one bad Summer following another.

During the Summer of 1899 the camp was taken from Laghelleren to Sanda, and even in July there was fast ice on the lakes of Taugevatn and Fagervatn.

The construction work was completed in 1901, and in that year the Summer was warm and sunny, and this made the work much easier.
In August a terrible storm of long duration forced the workers to stay indoors for 3 days.

THE PEACEFUL VALDRES REGION OF EASTERN NORWAY

Norway the Sublime

And in this land is the peace of dreams.
Peace cool and welcome as the summer rain
Over the lofty hills, or as icy streams
Threading the green valleys or the gentle plain
Peace all-enfolding as the sky and sand
Enfolding the beauty of this splendid land.

FINNISH TRAIN IN HELSINKI STATION WAITING TO DEPART

THE OFOTEN RAILWAY NEAR NARVIK

SPLENDOUR OF THE GEIRANGER FJORD

THE IDEAL MOUNTAIN RESORT—GEILO

FINNISH TRAIN IN WINTER'S FAIRYLAND

SLEIGHRIDE NEAR OSLO. WINTER TOO HAS ITS JOYS

"HAPPY DAYS ARE HERE AGAIN." LAPP MOTHER WITH CHILD.

Danish Tourist Office

HANS CHRISTIAN ANDERSEN'S HOUSE AT ODENSE ON THE MAIN LINE FROM ESBJERG TO COPENHAGEN. THE INTERESTING DANISH RAILWAY MUSEUM IS NEAR THE ODENSE STATION.

TRANSPORT ROADS.

One of the first essentials for the railway progress was to build roads for taking building material, tools, food, and provision for the workmen. The contractors Hornemann and Strom, who had built the Gravahals tunnel, built the transport way from Voss to Upsete. At that time Raundalen was completely cut off from Vossebygda. There was only a mere footpath over the Sverreskaret were King Sverre and his followers passed in 1177 to East Norway.

At the same time the railway's own engineers built a road the whole way from Aurlandsfjord right up to Myrdal. Up through the steep Myrdals mountain, from the farmstead at Kardal, through 17 curves, it was a gradient of 1 in 6. Ropes were also used to lift up the heavy goods straight up the mountain.

From Myrdal the road was continued further Eastwards, and in 1901 it reached Taugevanns point, the highest limit, before slowly descending. And even today you can sit back and relax and observe much of this winding road from the comfort of your train, climbing effortlessly over the high mountains, like a wonderful journey on a magic-carpet.

After the huts for the workers were connected by telephone cables to the valleys, construction work was commenced in a most hectic fashion. It was impossible to work amongst the high snowfalls of Winter, so all the energy was concentrated in the creation of tunnels. The men were almost isolated from the rest of the world, twice each week they eagerly read the letters from their families and nearest friends. One of the most steadfast postmen was Elling Hakestad, and his coming was always met with great jubilation.

'Varknipa' was the worst period, it was the parting of Winter from the end of March until the road could be opened. It was the unfortunate situation of having to live on tinned food, chiefly tinned milk and preserved fish, and everything had to be carried up by horses from the remote valleys.

WITH DRILL, DYNAMITE, AND DETERMINATION.

As soon as the Spring came, it became a rush of human-activity in the railways progressive construction. There was abundant labour, and most of the workers came from Eastern Norway, as soon as the ice began to melt from the lake Kroderen. Some of the workers were pennyless and poorly clothed, but as soon as they arrived for work, they were well looked after.

And what a fine example of human effort it was to sense the fervant activity during the height of the Summer. About a hundred horses were in a continuous journey between Fretheim with materials and tools of all kind.

There was also an increase of workers, including Swedes and Finns, and farmers sons from all parts of Norway. At Vatnahalsen, Hallingskeid, Finse, and Haugastol living quarters and shops were hastily erected, and the workers were given food and clothing which they paid for at a later date from some of their savings.

Most of the barracks were built for 12 men and a cook, sometimes larger huts could accommodate up to 40 men. At the height of activity 2,200 men were employed, and in general there was a high level of comradeship between the workers of all types. The work was done by piecework, and it was the foreman who arranged this with the engineer. The foreman was responsible for the quality of the work and the use of tools and dynamite.

The wages were very high for the turn of the century, and good workers earned as much as 8 Kronor a day. For lodging, fuel, and lighting the men only paid 4 Kroner a month, and food cost about 1.60 Kroner daily. The working hours were however, very long, about 10 hours daily, and often the younger men worked even longer on the long, light Summer days, when the red glow of sunset blended with the first signs of dawn. And when it snowed or rained heavily they could relax and take it easy until the following day.

At the approach of Autumn there was a constant feeling of unrest amongst the hired workers. The married men wanted to return to their families as soon as possible, the batchelors were more stable. With a well-filled wallet they said farewell to the snowy wastes of the mountains, to find work elsewhere in the larger towns of that beautiful land. Only the tunnel workers and engineers remained to fulfill their painstaking task.

61

EAST JOINS WEST – A TRIUMPH OF NORWEGIAN ENERGY AND ENTERPRISE.

The steady, tedious work of pushing the line ahead, both from the East and West, continued year after year. On the 7th October, 1907, the Western boundary by Ustaoset reached the Eastern sector which had been completed at an earlier date. And on the 9th October, the railway tracks were firmly united.

What a wonderful moment it was for Norway, the Railway, and those true Vikings who had worked and strived for so many years under severe conditions and intense cold to conquer the mountains and unite East and West in progress, richer friendship and understanding.

There was no official festivity that splendid October day, but a train with engineers and office workers from Myrdal and a train from Gulsvik met at Ustaoset. A few salutes from dynamite were improvised, the construction manager of the Western side, chief engineer H, Skavlen, gave a moving speech and joined in the jubilation with the workers and the chief engineer Peter Storen from the Eastern section.

Although the railway had been completed, the line was still not fit for regular use, owing to several deficencies. First and foremost, not enough snow-tunnels and snow-fences had been constructed. The line between Roa and Gulsvik was not ready, and added to this King Winter still reigned triumphant. The Employment minister gave instructions to prepare for the opening, and personnel were employed, many of whom had little experience of mountain conditions and were not prepared for trouble.

When the train reached Haugastol, it became trapped in the snow, a snow-plough from Finse was ordered, but this also could not make enough progress. So the opening-train had to return to Gulsvik. Things went from bad to worse, and it was not long before the whole line was buried in the deep snow.

After one and a half month's painstaking work which cost 50,000 kroner, the track was at last fit for use. And at Whitsum 1908 a delayed train made it's lucky trip, and this gave much encouragement to all concerned. And during the next few months 4 new locomotives were in use, and 2 rotating snow-ploughs. It took about 21 hours to cover the 585 kilometers (about 350 miles) on the still incomplete line., from

Oslo to Bergen.

On 10th June the first ordinary train was able to make the whole trip from East to West. The train first left Oslo (called Kristiania) V. to Kroderen, then one boarded at Kroderen, one of the two steamers, 'Norefjell' or 'Kroderen' and the train journey was resumed at Gulsvik, And what a difficult journey it was. There were no dining-cars on the train, so on arrival at Finse there was a great demand for food of all kinds. Yet in spite of hazards and late arrivals at destinations, it was indeed a splendid victory for the Norwegian Railways.

The line between Gulsvik and Roa was ready on 1st November 1909, and thus everything was perfect for the official opening of the Bergen Railway. Although the season was not the most suitable, the opening was celebrated in a most hearty manner 3 or 4 days in succession.

First a train was sent from Bergen to the capital, and the next day another train left in the opposite direction, with the King, Government, and Storting, foreign diplomats and newspaper reporters, while in a third-class wagon nearest the locomotive were those fine men, the hard-working engineers who built the pioneer line with spirit and determination.

At Voss the King was hailed Welcome by the people of Voss and his Majesty said the Bergen Railway was the people's masterpiece. Three thousand people waved Farewell before the train continued on it's way to Bergen, and here the enthusiasm reached it's climax.

The King gave a lengthy speech, with strong, steadfast, and sincere praise to those dedicated leaders (and I might add lovers of progress and the dignity of mankind), such as Lars Hille, Thorbjorn Lekve, who worked around Finse, Norway's highest station, H. Skavlan, who died at the young age of 56, before the official opening, and Peter Storen and J. Fasting.

The following day, 29th November, 1909, the train went for the second time over the Nygards bridge, heading East, while the cannons thundered from the Bergenshus fortress. It was also typical weather to be experienced in Norway this time of the year, a drop in temperature along the Sorfjord, a snow-storm at Voss, and a driving storm across the high mountain fells.

'The Bergen-Line, the Railway of a thousand disappointments, a thousand obstacles, and a thousand hopes,' was at last open for use.

IT WAS A VIKING SAGA OF HARD WORK, TENACITY, BRILLIANT CALCULATION, PATIENCE, AND ABOVE ALL HUMAN COMRADESHIP.

Rails across the Mountain fells.

It cost fifty million Kroner to build the railway, and two and a half million working days.

Alone in the mountain area, two million cubic meters of rock were extracted, and about 700,000 cubic meters of dynamite were used. Considering the terrain, extreme climatic conditions, and great differences in altitude, it was quite inexpensive. One also takes into account that the initial construction was primitive compared with more modern standards. The railway was simple and planned without too many complex details, short tracks at the stations, steep gradients, and sharp curves. The shortest curve had a radius of only 250 meters.

After a short time it was clearly understood that to deal with the ever increasing traffic on the line, far more powerful locomotives would be essential. In the initial stages, light rails were in use, 25 kilos per meter on the lower land, and 30 kilos across the mountains and between Roa and Honefoss. Between 1911-21 all the rails were replaced by 35 kilo rails. And in the Gravahalsen tunnel the rails were worn out and so had to be replaced. So over the high mountains 49 kilos became the normal. Today it has been further increased to 49 kilos over the whole length of the Bergen Line, and an axis pressure of 18 tons.

It was not only the mountains which presented the biggest problem, but the steep slopes, and those on the Western side were truly formidable. The biggest obstacle was 45 kilometers East from Voss, the Urhovdi mountain, far too steep to be surmounted from the outside. The only solution was to tunnel through the sheer rock for 5 kilometers (3 miles). Many discussions were made before the Stortinget decided to build it in 1894. Many tenders were presented, both from Norway and abroad, and it was the combined efforts of the engineers, Thorvald Strom, Kristen Hornemann who, together with their steadfast teams, made it a success of patient labour.

One cold, grey October day in 1895, the very first work was commenced at the Western entrance to the tunnel. Here the barracks and workshops were situated, and the contractors settled in to live. Ordinary tools were alone not sufficient to make steady progress, so soon hydraulic and pneumatic drilling machines were used.

On the Eastern side, hand boring tools were quickly replaced by machine-boring. The day's average progress was about 2 meters (6.5 ft) each day, and about 130 to 150 men were employed. It was not easy to find experienced men, and in 1900 Italian tunnelers were brought to teach the less skilled Norwegians. But the Italians were not used to drilling in such hard rocks under such severe weather conditions, so they were sent home.

The work on the tunnel went according to plan, and there were few serious accidents. On one occasion, in 1901 there was a landfall on the Eastern side, and 20 men were cut off for 5 hours before being rescued.

During the Summer of 1902 the work forces of East and West approached each other, and the 6th July, the great day had arrived, when they finally met. Many important personalities met that day, general director Nysom, the railway manager Fleischer, minister of state Lovland, and officials such as Hroar Olsen and J.L. Mowinckel from Bergen. And to note the accuracy of this gigantic feat, only 4 centimeters (2 inches) in a vertical direction, out of line.

Altogether the work had cost not more than 3 million Kroner, a relatively low price, and perhaps just as important, the trains were able to pass through the tunnel several months prior to the estimated time.

The longest tunnel on the Eastern side is the Haversting tunnel between Sokna and Orgenvika. It is 2,311 meters in length (About 1½ miles) in a straight line, with 500 meters (about 1,600 ft.) of mountain above the roof of the tunnel. It took 5 years to drill through the hard rock, and hand boring tools were used.

The creation of the 1,593m. long Reinungtunnel between Myrdal and Hallingskeid was met with problems. For to avoid sharp curves it was not possible to tunnel deep into the mountain, and so often clay, stones, and rocks would drop down. One day a huge amount of debris filled most of the tunnel, and it took months to clear it.

ACROSS VALLEYS AND RIVERS, RAVINES
AND STREAMS.

Thanks to the wild terrain, mountains and deep green valleys, there are no less than 300 bridges between Oslo and Bergen. And here the Norwegians showed their true spirit, they made the bridges strong, and at the same time beautiful to blend with their immediate surroundings.

Before the Bergen Line was built, iron bridges were the rule, but now stone bridges were found to be efficient and scenic. Iron bridges still exist, such as those over the Ustedalselva, over the Sokna, and over the Randselva (Elva denotes Bridges in Norwegian), with a free span width of 54 meters (about 180 ft.)

Perhaps first and foremost we could mention the splendid and imposing bridge over the river Bregna at Honefoss. It is 215 meters long (660 ft.) and has 8 spans. 5,000 cubic meters of stone were used in it's construction, transported from a quarry near Drammen. It became important too, both for style and elegance and being the longest stone bridge in Northern Europe.

Another bridge, almost equally worthy of attention, was the Svenkerudbrua, which crosses the Hallingdalselva just South of Gol in a lofty span of 44 meters. Then there is the bridge across the rushing torrent at Kleivevannsoset, between Hallingskeid and Myrdal. It is so beautiful and cleverly built, that it has the appearance of growing out from the rocky fells. The bridge over the Strande river at Voss is a sheer delight to the eyes.

These bridges, strong, graceful, and symmetric give added joy to those fortunate passengers who enjoy the comfort of travel on Norwegian Railways, and are a lasting tribute to those who built the railways.

These bridges span the valleys, rivers, cascading streams, and rocky outcrops in splendour and silent joy, almost to remind one of the grandeur of the Norwegian landscape, and the harmony, joy and love of the music of Edvard Grieg.

Night and day, Winter and Summer, they retain their splendour in just the same way as the silver birch, simple and slender, yet full of grace, harmony, representing the true perfection of beauty.

FROM STEAM TO ELECTRICITY.

Almost 60 years after the rails were laid on the Bergen Railway, a new transformation took place. This time it was not new rails, but electrification.

In 1952 the Stortinget decided that it was time to put electric power in use on the Bergen Line. During the preparations meteorologists and landslide specialists were much in demand, for the problem of ice and heavy coverings of snow was ever present. A special experiment with the use of electricity in the high mountains took place at Larsbu in the neighbourhood of Finse.

It was decided that the 100 kilometer (62 mile) stretch of line from Geilo to Mjofjell could be considered as the special high-mountain stretch, and 87 kilometers of this of extra importance. The contact masts which generally were 60 meters apart, were only 40 meters apart. The weight of the contact lines was increased from 1,125 kg. to 1,300 kg. Wooden masts were not in use, it was usually concrete, and, where landslides were common, steel masts were erected. On the latter, bolts were fitted in such a condition that, in case of a landslide, the mast would be moved, but the electric power lines would still remain in position. And in various districts reserve masts can be quickly put in use.

In order to keep snow and ice from collecting on the elctric contacts, means are used to warm them up, whenever necessary. In particular this is to be seen between Finse and Myrdal, and a special transformer for this is to be found at Finse.

On the contact leads there is a 15,000 voltage power, and sometimes it is necessary to repair the line. Then the power is shut off on certain stretches, and a reserve line is put into use until the repair has been finished.

There are special repair workshops for this in various places along the line, such as Honefoss, Nesbyen, Al, Finse, Myrdal, Dale and Arna. At Finse the equipment through necessity is great and varied, as also a high-powered locomotive for snow-clearing. And in the tunnels it would be far too dangerous to enlarge the roof, so the lines were put underground.

For the steady supply of power on the Bergen Line 5 transformers give the necessary power. The transformers reduce the power from the initial supply from 60,000 to 15,000 volts.

The Line was put into use by electricity in stages. First the Voss Line in 1954, Oslo, Roa, Honefoss in 1961, Honefoss-Al, 1962, Al-Ustaoset in 1963. And in December 1964 the last part, from Ustaoset to Voss was electrified, so the whole line was electrified.

SNOW – AN ETERNAL STRUGGLE WITH THE ELEMENTS.

In Central Europe there are many lines which reach a much greater altitude than the Bergen Line, but they are all below the tree-limit. The Bergen Line reaches about 1,300 meters (about 4,300 ft) and West from Geilo to Mjolfjell the line passes desolate and barren tracts of wild and windswept mountains. For 100 kilometers the region is a vast, untamed wilderness, surmounted by the mountain massifs of Hallingskarvet and Hardangerjoklen.

The snow is the eternal enemy of the trains on the high mountain stretches, especially with high winds. To win this struggle special material protection and terrific power to move the snow is necessary. Systematic planning is essential to keep the line open under all conditions. Regular snow-measurements were already taken as early as 1884, and on the highest settlements on both East and West sides meteorlogical stations were a splendid help in helping the railway personnel.

Snow attacks in 2 different ways. Avalanches are a great danger, both to regular traffic, and to the safety of the trains. In this case, it is vital to build a strong overhead protection above the line. These are very expensive to build and constantly maintain. In some special instances, it has been found prudent to build special tunnels as a strong and permanent protection. Between Kleivebrua and the 5 kilometers to Myrdal the line is for most of it's length in a complete tunnel. The tunnel is so near the mountain side that several openings have been built, and several breathtaking views can be taken over the mountain lakes of Seltuft and Reinunga, deep in the valley below.

Landslides are dangerous, but with time, it is soon found where and when to expect them, and then proper protection can be implimented before they suddenly occur.

But the most dangerous element of all is the snow-storm, for it can come with often unexpected rapidity and in quite a short period of time cause great havoc to regular traffic. Yet people with experience and knowledge can expect where to find the heaviest falls, and the wind direction is a vital clue. Snowshields, tunnels, and windbreaks are fortified and altered to take into account the snow conditions. Often great effort is needed to make the construction stand the power of the storm and heavy weight of the snow, and even this is sometimes of little avail. In 1966-67 a total of 1,300 meters of building protection was destroyed. That Winter the snow was so deep that up to a depth of 18 meters (57 ft.) was measured against one of the protective fences.

The railway men are continually working with methods of using the most effective and efficient means of constructing protective structures. And as the Summers are short and often unreliable, it is necessary to work as well as possible, so prefabrication is becoming even more prominent. There is a total of 28 kilometers (17 miles) of snow-covers on the Bergen Line, not always very popular for the passengers, but essential for the train's punctuality.

Snowshields are everywhere in use to protect the line from snow piling up, and during the Winter of 1966-67 various types of shields were used near Finse to improve their usefulness. They are seldom longer than 100 meters, and are usually 5 to 7 meters high (15 to 21 ft.)

FINSE – THE TRACK WORKERS HEADQUARTERS.

This is the highest station on the Bergen Line, and is also the headquarters of those hardy, reliable, and hospitable men who keep the line open throughout the year, regardless of weather conditions. Of the 100 people who live at Finse, nearly all are connected with the railway. And here the line inspector has the responsibility of controlling the great length of railway from Reimegrad in the West to Honefoss in the East.

A huge assembly of large and small material is here assembled and carefully serviced for continuous use, from electrical components to powerful snow-ploughs. And in Summer, Finse and the immediate surroundings are a hive of human activity, repairing the line, strengthening the snow-fences, and many other activities aimed at improving the safety, speed, and reliability of the railway.

Once Winter comes, often as early as the end of October or early November, the eternal struggle with wind, ice and snow begins. There is much to be done, repairing the track or strengthening protecting supports or using the snow-plough to clear the track from heavy snow drifts. If the snow driven from the track is so high that it collects in a huge pile adjoining the track, it is necessary to use a snow scraper to drive these piles inwards, later to be forced far outwards by a powerful rotator.

During the long, dark evenings, when the sky is clear and the stars twinkle like bright diamonds overhead, those tough individuals are able to relax a little, to read or write letters or play cards. It is so quiet that you could almost hear the silence, and an approaching train can be heard far away at a distance of several kilometers.

Those fortunate individuals on the night express relax in their warm compartments, drink coffee and enjoy a delicious sandwich from one of the helpful waiters or waitresses. The train speeds on through the night, surrounded by the mountains, dark forested valleys, and snow covered fields.

And we look back with gratitude and warm friendship towards the many thousands of hard-working Norwegians who have used their ideas, ideals, and initiative to make this unique train journey a lasting enjoyment and splendid experience.

BODÖ – END STATION OF THE NORDLANDS RAILWAY

Some Important Facts abouth the Swedish State Railways.

Locomotive first put into operation — 1856.

Railway network

Stockholm — Gothenburg	opened 8 November 1862	465Km(290 miles)
Falkoping—Nassjo—Malmo	opened 1 December 1864	381Km(270 miles)
Laxa — Norwegian frontier	opened 19 June 1871	209Km(166 miles)
Katrineholm — Nassjo	opened 23 November 1874	217Km(140 miles)
Stockholm — Krylbo	opened 22 July 1882	748Km(470 miles)
—Ostersund — Storlien		
Lulea — Gallivare	opened for goods transport 1888	204Km(120 miles)
Bracke —Boden	opened 6 August 1894	630Km(420 miles)
Gallivare — Riksgransen	opened 15 November 1902	230Km(135 miles)

Actual distances in present day Rail Network

Stockholm — Gavle — Bollnas — Storlien	709Km(425 miles)
Stockholm — Gavle — Bollnas — Riksgransen	1502Km(940 miles)
Stockholm — Malmo	599Km(360 miles)
Stockholm — Charlottenberg	

Largest Bridges

	Type	Longest span	Height above water
1929 Arsta bridge	Steel arch	150 meters	28 meters
1912 Forsmo bridge	" "	104 meters	45 meters
1952 Vindelalven	Concrete arch	112 meters	30 meters

(The longest bridge is the Gotaalv bridge, at Gothenburg, 858 meters, which consts of many small, long spans — next the Arsta bridge — 753m.)

Highest points.

Storlien	592 meters above sea level	(1800 ft.)
Riksgransen	521 meters above sea level	(1600 ft.)
Nassjo	293 meters above sea level	(900 ft.)

The highest point is at 601 meters, near Storlien, latitude 63 degrees North
Highest point in South Sweden, 315 meters, between Nassjo and Grimstorp
Lapland Line's highest point, 551 meters, between Harra and Fjallasen
67 degrees North.

Work was also commenced from Stockholm in 1857, and already by 1860 the line to Sodertalje was completed.

After 1860 the development proceeded at a remarkable speed, and here are some of the achievements.

Lines	Region served	Opened for traffic	
West	Stockholm — Gothenburg	November	1826
	Hallsberg — Orebro	August	1826
South	Falkoping — Nassjo — Malmo	December	1864
Northwest	Laxa — Norwegian frontier	June	1871
Connection	Stockholm C — Stockhom S	July	1871
East	Katrineholm — Nassjo	November	1874
North	Stockholm — Krylbo — Storvik	September	1875

The continuation of the line in Northern Sweden was a gigantic task, owing to the sparse population, great distances between towns, large rivers and in some places mountainous terrain. Added to this was the length and severity of the Winters.

The stretch, Storvik—Ange was opened in 1881, and in 1882 the central line was declared open by King Oscar at Storlien, on the Norwegian frontier. And by 1894 the railway across Northern Norrland was finished, with Boden as it's terminus. Boden is a vital connection with the iron-ore line, Lulea — Gallivare.

The iron-ore Line, which was commenced in 1884 by an English company, was taken over by the state in 1891. By 1898 it was lengthened to the west, reaching Riksgransen and Narvik, and was opened by the king at Riksgransen in 1903.

Besides the main lines, a series of branch lines were put into use, such as Krylbo—Frovi (1900), Jarna—Norrkoping (1915), and the important side lines to the coastal towns in Norrland.

The Inland railway, serving the remote area of the inner area of Norrland from Sveg, northwards to Gallivare, was finished in 1937. And the very latest line was completed in 1964, from Kiruna to Svappavaara.

The total length of lines is 11,400 kilometers (About 7,000 miles and of this total, 31% was built by the state, and 69% by private initiative. In 1879 the state took over the first private railway,and by 1939 it was decided that all the lines should be state owned.

Owing to several economic factors, such as private cars, and heavy transport lorries, the total length has been reduced to 12,800 Km. by 1968. And most of the important lines have a double track, in sharp contrast to the Norwegian Railways, which are mostly single-track.

Right from the beginning the connecting line through Stockholm was double-tracked, and by the turn of the century work on making the lines also double-tracked was started.

THE DEVELOPMENT OF SWEDISH RAILWAYS.

A clever and enterprising Englishman, Thomas Stawford, built the first railway in Sweden. It was horse-drawn and was used for transport between the coal-mines and harbour at Hoganas and was initiated in 1798.

The construction of railways, mostly only over small sections, was continued during the following century, especially in the province of Varmland. With horse-drawn transport and connections with the chain of lakes it was possible to form a reliable link from the extreme North of Varmland near the border of Dalarna across Filipstads area to the shores of Lake Vanern. Persbergs mines also used a convenient route to the lake by Christinehamns Railway. It was founded in 1850 and was 23 years in use.

Sweden's first railway company, the Frykstads Jernvags Aktie Bolag, was formed in 1849, thanks to the well guided energy of Mr. Claes Adelskold. This formidable Swede, with tremendous energy and insight built railways for a total of 26 years, and planned the construction of 3,000 kilometers (1,800 miles) of rail, he personally supervised the construction of over 700 Km. (420 miles) of track.

It was Count Adolf Eugene von Rosen who gave the necessary initiative to build railways on a large scale. During a visit to England, the true pioneer of railways, he became convinced that railways linking the larger centres of population and industry would be essential to progress in Sweden's economy. In 1845 he was granted permission to build the railways he envisaged, but owing to lack of financial backing, he was at first limited to link Lake Vanern to Hjalmaren, and later 2 of Sweden's largest lakes, Vanern and Malaren.

The result was the formation of the company 'Koping-Hults Jarnvag' and his enthusiastic attitude was greatly welcomed and encouraged. The first step towards a more active railway growth was taken in 1852, when the director for the topographical institute, General Major Karl Akrell, was given the welcome task of finding out a system of railways for the land., and in 1853—54, the government would be responsible for constructing the more important lines, while minor lines could be built by private companies, with official permission.

The highest direction for railway pioneering was given to Nils Eriksson, a brother to the inventor John Eriksson. Work began on 1st April, 1855, and the first stretch, Gothenburg—Jonsered, and Malmo—Lund, was opened on 1st December, 1856. Other lines were almost simultaneously opened, such as the line from Orebro to Nora, Koping — Hults Railway, and 1856 can be said to have been the Birthday of the Swedish railways.

At the same time as Nils Eriksson was engaged in his vital work, a committee made about 500 proposals for various main lines. But the interest was centred around Gothenburg, and work commenced from both towns.

In the beginning, only the areas near Malmo and Stockholm were concerned, and it was only towards the end of the thirties work was done to improve the lines Stockholm —Gothenburg and Katrineholm —Malmo. The former became completely double-tracked by 1958, the latter in 1964. Some parts of other lines are double-tracked on certain stretches, e.g. Hallsberg—Frovi, and sections of the Norrland. Railways.

Much energy and finance has been used to improve the strength and durability of the railway, to deal with greater speeds and heavier wagons, thus enabling more frequent trains. Remote control plays a vital role in making the trains safer and faster.

To further ensure the utmost efficiency, the administration has been divided into eleven districts, and the towns which are concerned are, Malmo, Vaxjo, Boras, Goteborg, Norrkoping, Stockholm, Orebro, Gavle, Sundsvall, Umea, and Lulea.

THE STEAM EPOCH

The very first steam locomotive was constructed by the Englishman Richard Trevithick, and it was initially used in 1804, for a short time on a mine in Wales, it had only one cylinder, and the driving power was transmitted by means of a cog-wheel.

It was closely followed by another locomotive constructed by John Blenkinsop, in 1812. This was a much stronger and practical machine, being a 2 cylinder model, and more complexly built.

William Hedley built a still better model, in 1813, by the most appropriate name of 'Puffing Billy', and this locomotive was the true forerunner of present day models.

Yet the most important man in the history of railway pioneers was George Stevenson. He built his first locomotive in 1814, and continued many years in a most determined manner to improve the development of his ideal and idea. His son, Robert, was educated to a machine engineer, and in 1823 the firm of Robert Stevenson was established, to build locomotives.

Timothy Hackworth was made the director, and one of the first products was 'Locomotion', which was put into daily use in 1825, and it was George Stevenson who gave it it's trail run in September of the first year, between Stockton and Darlington.

The railway line was built by Stevenson, and was the World's first railway used for commercial traffic. It was used only for transport of goods, as a train which carried passengers was pulled by horses which maintained a greater speed.

When the railway between Liverpool and Manchester was under construction, George Stevenson was again designated to be the works director. Naturally this encouraged Stevenson to do his utmost and he influenced the administrations to have a competition to find out which locomotive was most suitable.

In the competition, which took place between 6—14 October, 1829 Robert Stevenson's locomotive 'Rocket', beat the Swedish inventor's John Eriksson's model 'Novelty' and Timothy Hackwork's 'San Pareil' both which had to stop the run owing to a breakdown.

Timothy Bursta II received a second prize for his machine 'Perseverance', which unfortunately could not reach the designated speed.

This historical contest at Rainhill was the forming of a breakthrough into rail transport as a definate programme. The Liverpool and Manchester Railway, which was opened in 1830 was the first railway where both goods and personnel traffic were transported by steam power.

TRAIN CONSTRUCTION IN SWEDEN.

England was enterprising and capable enough under the beginning of the 19th century to supply many European lands with locomotives of various types and sizes. Even when Sweden imported her first locomotive in 1853.

Named the 'Forstlingen', it was presented to Frederik Sundler, director for the Norbergs Railway construction. Munktells second locomotive 'Frystad' was built in 1855 for Frystad's Railway.

It was in the 1860's when the Swedish locomotive construction gained momentum. Motala Workshop supplied it's first locomotive in 1862, the 'Carlsund' to the mining company Vieille Montagne at Ammeberg, and it was named after the workshop's director. The second locomotive 'Motala' left the workshop during the following year.

Nydqvist and Holm Trollhattan began in 1865 it's locomotive construction with several locomotives for the Uddevalla — Vanersborg —Herrljunga Railway. The first was named 'Trollhattan', and the same name was given to the firm's first locomotive supplied to the Swedish State Railways in 1868.

The first Swedish made locomotive delivered to the Swedish State Railways was in 1861, by Nykoping's mechanical workshop, which built eight locomotives between 1861 and 1863. Five of these were supplied to the Swedish State Railways. The following companies also built locomotives in a large quantity.

Vagn & Maskinfabriks AB	—	Falun
AB Atlas	—	Stockholm
Kristinehamns Mekaniska Verkstad		
Halsingborgs Mekaniska Verkstad		
Ljunggrens Verkstad AB	—	Kristianstad

LOCOMOTIVE TYPE DEVELOPMENT WITH THE SWEDISH STATE RAILWAYS.

When the initial railways were constructed, two already used locomotives from England, Ajax and Titan, were imported to be put into immediate use. This was closely followed by the purchase of 6 locomotives from the Manchester firm of Beyer, Peacock and Co., the first three were named Prins Carl, Prins Oaskar and Prins August and were used in the Malmo region. Locomotives 4 to 6 were named Norden, Sverige, and Goteborg and were sent to Gothenburg.

Between the years 1856 and 1873 a total of 45 locomotives were purchased from the British firm and in addition Swedish firms.

For the fast trains on the West Railway, completed in 1862, locomotves were ordered from the British firm. They were called Litt A (Little A) and from 1863 to 1873, 32 locomotives of this type, chiefly from England were supplied. They did a fine job of work before being replaced by more powerful engines needed to pull heavier loads.

At the same time as passenger trains were put into operation, it was necessary to supply heavy goods trains. 14 locomotives were supplied from Beyer, Peacock, and Co., from 1863 to 1865, and between 1866 and 1874 a total of 51 more powerful locomotives were put into action. Some of these were supplied from Britain, others by the Swedish firm of

Nydqvist and Holm.

From 1874 onwards, new locomotives were carefully built, some for passenger trains, others for combined passenger and good trains. The demand for even more powerful locomotives grew at an ever increasing rate, so in 1874-75 twelve locomotives were dispatched from Sharp, Stewart and Co., in Manchester. In 1886 the Swedes also built five powerful passenger locomotives, and shortly after locomotives were constructed to be even more powerful.

At the turn of the century, the demand for locomotives was so great, that neither the Swedish or Euopean workshops could deliver them within sufficient time. The Swedish State Railways ordered 10 locomotives from the American firm Richmond Locomotive and Machine Works, which were supplied in 1899.

The exploitation of the huge reserves of iron-ore at Kiruna, in Swedish Lapland, brought many new developments and challenges. A locomotive was needed, which was capable of pulling a train with a total weight of 1,000 tons, a tremendous weight. And the locomotives had to be built to protect the personnel from the extreme cold and rapid temperature fluctuations.

I could continue to give a more lengthy story of the long and progressive chain of development of the Swedish State Railways, but it is here, in the heart of Lapland, where I would like to finish this fascinating railway epoch.

The Swedish railways began on a very small scale, with primitive conditions and locomotives which, by modern standards, would seem more like minature models. And yet, by hard work, determination, and a truly pioneer spirit, the Swedish State Railways is today something to regard rather with pride and admiration. Fast ferry ships transport passengers, cars, and trains to Denmark and Germany, and happy travellers like myself can relax in comfort any hour of the day or night.

I have travelled the entire length and breadth of Sweden by train, from Ystad, a small idyllic town situated on the Southern extreme, by the blue waters of the Baltic, to Riskgransen, well above the Arctic Cricle, where only dwarf birches and tiny mountain plants grow during the brief, short Summer.

And I have experienced the grandeur of the silent forests which grow over a distance of several hundred miles across Northern and Central Sweden.

On a warm Summer's eve I have left Stockholm, bound for Jamtland, that splendid province of lonely mountain fells, majestic forests, rushing rivers, quiet lakes, and homely villages. Even the ever-present memory of arriving in Gothenburg on a wet, windy Autumn day, still gives me that feeling of homesickness for the Eternal North.

I can clearly visualise glancing out of the window on a cold clear night, and seeing the tall outlines of the forest trees under a sky bright with a multitude of stars shining bright.

Travelling by train in Sweden, in Spring, Summer, Autumn, or Winter, is an experience never to be missed, it is the gateway to a fuller, happier life, new experiences, and many long-lasting memories.

INTERESTING FACTS AND FIGURES OF THE SCANDINAVIAN LANDS.

DENMARK.

Denmark has the mildest climate of all the Scandinavian lands being on roughly the same latitude as Scotland, and consisting chiefly of islands and the Jutland peninsular. Indeed, no point is further than 30 miles from the coast, so the presence of the sea has a very marked effect, making the Summers somewhat cooler and the Winters much milder, although being nearer the land mass of Northern Europe tends to influence the land to some extent.

Only seldom does the sea ever freeze, and this is on the Baltic region. The average January temperature is minus 0.3 degrees c. or just under freezing, the July temperature 17 degrees c. (62 F.), almost identical to London. The number of annual frost days ranges from about 70 on the coast, to 120 in the interior.

The landscape is very low, rather similar to Holland, the highest point is Yding Skovhoj, 173 meters (568 ft.) There are many lakes on the fertile undulating plains, the largest being Lake Arreso, 40 sq.km. (16 sq. miles)

Of the 482 islands comprising Denmark, 99 are inhabited. The population is just under 5 million, with about 100 to the square kilometer, as against 11 in Norway and 17 in Sweden. The language is quite distinct from

English, German, French and other European languages but has much in common with the Swedish and Norwegian languages to be fairly well understood by other Scandinavian, apart from the Finns.

Length — North — South about 360 km. (225 miles)
Width — East — West about 400 km. (250 miles)

Total length of coastline 7,474km. (4,645 miles)

The land frontier with Germany is a mere 68 km. (42 miles) and the land area is 43,043 sq.km. (16,619 sq.miles) The longest inlet is Limfjord 180 km. (112 miles), and the longest river is the Gudena 160 km (100 miles).

SOUNDS AND BELTS

The Great Belt is 15 km. (9 miles) i.e. Storebaelt.
The Sound (Oresund) 4 km. (2.5 miles)
Little Belt (Lillebaelt) 0.66 km. (.4 miles)

The largest city is Greater Copenhagen, with approx. 1,400,000 people, followed by Arhus, 195,000, Odense 145,000, Alborg 130,000, Esbjerg 65,000, and Randers 54,000.

Denmark's chief industry is farming with the export of daily produce and meat taking pride of place. (With humour) Denmark boasts of having more pigs to keep than human beings, well over the 5 million mark. In post war years there has been a rapid development of engineering products, ship-building, and the Danish merchant navy sails to all corners of the World.

Denmark is also responsible for the administration of Greenland, the largest island in the World, with the huge land area of 2,175,000 sq. kilometers (840,000 sq. miles). Of this area, only 340,000 sq. km about 132,000 sq. miles, is ice-free, and only half of this can be classified as inhabited, chiefly in the extreme South West. The Northern tip is latitude 83 degrees N., Cape Morris, and the Southern tip is Cape Farewell, 60 degrees N. about the same as Stockholm, Helsinki, and Oslo.

The mountains are extremely high, as is the depth of the gigantic ice-cap. The highest peak is Gunnbjorns Fjaeld (3,700 meters — 12,000 ft.) and at it's thickest the ice-cap measures 2,000 meters, about 6,500 ft.

Greenland's population is a mere 38,000 partly Eskimo, but chiefly made up of Greenlanders, a Mongoloid-Caucasian cross between Danes and Eskimos.

Sealing and hunting are still carried on, but today most of the hardy inhabitants partake in modern fishing of cod, halibut and shrimps., and even sheep farming has become popular.

The capital is Godthab, followed by Frederikshab and Holsteinsborg, which are all busy fishing ports. Greenland was first inhabited by the adventurous Vikings, a thousand year ago, at the same time as the Eskimos moved in from the North.

The Faroe islands are situated in the North Atlantic, approx. latitude 62 degrees North. Hence the climate is rather harsh, in January the average temperature is plus 3 degrees c. (38 degrees F.) while the July mean temperature is only 10 degrees c. (50 degrees). The rain-fall is high, 159 cm. (63 inches) and the fogs are both frequent and intense. So the vegetation is extremely poor, amongst the rocky hills the grasses support only sheep and a few cattle, trees are very rare. The inhabitants number some 36,000 and their language resembles modern Norwegian and Icelandic. Fishing is the main occupation, and Thorshavn, with a population of 8,000 is the capital. Since 1948 the Faroes have become self-governing, with their own flag.

ÅNDALSNES — A QUIET TOWN IN A HEAVENLY SETTING

NORWAY.

Norway forms the Western part of the Scandinavian peninsular, of which it covers about 40%. The land area is 323,883 sq.km. (125,000 sq. miles) and of this 72% is mountains, lakes, and glaciers, 25% forest, and a mere 3% is suitable for agriculture. It's greatest length, from Lindesnes in the extreme South to the North Cape, high up above the Arctic Circle, is 1,800 kilometers, (1,100 miles), while the total coastline is 20,000 kilometers, 12,000 miles, as far as London is from New Zealand. It's longest frontier is with Sweden, 1,200 miles, followed by Finland, 445 miles, and The Soviet Union, 122 miles.

Along it's immense coastline there are some 50,000 islands, and of these, only 2,000 are inhabited. The Capital, situated on latitude 60 degrees North, is as far North as Central Canada and Alaska, while the most Northern town, Hammerfest, is almost 71 Degrees North. The Arctic Circle, 66½ degrees N. passes just North of the bustling industrial town of Mo i Rana, so Northern Norway is well known as the land of the Midnight Sun, as here the sun never sets during the longest days.

Norway is extremely mountainous, for 80% is above 150 meters (about 500 ft.), and the average altitude is 500 meters, about 1,560 ft. Amongst the rugged, windswept high plateaux are numerous lakes, and Lake Hornindalsvatn is the deepest in Europe. Another interesting factor is that the mountains slope down very swiftly towards the West, some of the slopes by the deep fjords being almost vertical, they generally slope very gradually towards the East and the Swedish frontier. If one takes the train from Ostersund, in Central Sweden, the gradient to Are and Storlien is so gradual as to pass almost unnoticed, yet from Storlien to the Norwegian coast along the Stjordal valley is often extremely steep.

A HELSINKI BOUND TRAIN BESIDE ONE HEADING FOR VASA, AT SEINÄJOKI.

AN EXPRESS TO HELSINKI AT ROVANEMI, JUST SOUTH OF THE ARCTIC
CIRCLE.

BODEN, AN IMPORTANT RAIL JUNCTION IN NORTHERN SWEDEN.

THE FINE CITY OF GAVLE HAS SWEDEN'S EXCELLENT
RAILWAY MUSEUM AND NEARBY, STREETS WHERE TIME
SEEMS TO HAVE STOOD STILL.

FRYCKSTAD IN HONOURABLE RETIREMENT AT GAVLE.
BUILT IN 1855, IT WORKED ON THE FRYKEN-KLARALVEN RAILWAY.

HELSINKI-IMATRA TRAIN CROSSING KORIA BRIDGE OVER ONE OF
FINLAND'S MANY BEAUTIFUL WATERWAYS.

FINNISH STATE RAILWAYS

The Dovre mountain chain, which runs chiefly in an East-West direction, divides the country into a Northern and Southern region, while the latter is divided by the Langfjellene mountains into an Eastern and Western section. The long mountain chain 'Kjolen' runs in a North-South direction along a greater part of the Norwegian-Swedish frontier.

Glaciers and rivers of the Ice Age have cut valleys into the mountains long and sloping towards East and South, and short and steep towards the West. They are continued by the Fjords often very narrow and yet penetrating a long way inland, even as much as 183 kilometers (115 miles) as in the case of the Sogne Fjord.

The total number of glaciers in Norway is 1,700 and they cover an area of 1,300 square miles.

In the West the highest falls are situated, while towards the East the rivers are both greater in volume, and generally much slower, as in the example of the River Glomma Norways greatest river, with a length of 380 miles. Mardalsfossen has a straight fall of 974 ft.

FAUNA AND FLORA

Norways flora is much richer than what might be expected so far North, with severe frost in the interior during the long Winters, yet there are about 2,000 species. Most of the plants are similar to those found elsewhere in Northern Europe, only a few of the mountain plants are peculair to Norway.

Forest covers about a quarter of the landscape, and the most common trees are spruce and pine, followed by birch and a few deciduous trees, the mountain birch is extremely hardy and grows up to about 1,000 meters above sea level (over 3,000 ft.). Towards the South East the vegetation is most prolific, and here are to be found huge forests, which form the basis of the timber industry.

Wild berries grow in the woodlands, particularly cranberries and blueberries. Cloudberries, little known elsewhere, apart from Finnish Lapland, are picked in the remote mountains, and make a very popular and rather expensive delicacy.

Along the long, stretching Western coastline fish are abundant
and form a highly important industry, including canning and export.
In Stavanger many students from all over the World study the canning
industry at a special college. Most of the bear population is almost
extinct, but many idealists, especially members of the Norwegian
Nature Preservation Society, are doing much to preserve wild-life
and form much needed nature reserves. In the South and Trondelag
area Elk are very prolific, while in the extreme North, in the
plateau Finnmark region, reindeer give a source of livelihood
to the Laplanders.

Otters, Lynx, fox abound, while game birds, such as ptarmigan, are
found almost everywhere, as do trout and salmon in many of the
wilder rivers. On the high, rocky cliffs of the West Coast, thousands
of sea-birds nest. In addition, many of Norway's birds are migratory,
living in more Northern parts for much of the year.

NATIONAL PARKS.

The Norwegians are extremely fortunate in having access to
vast forests, unspoilt mountains, and a multitude of rivers and
lakes. Altogether, about 96 per cent is open to the public.

But since the war there have been increasing demands of a growing
population for housing, roads, and hydro-electric plants, which tend
to be detrimental to the environment.

Many individuals have been so alarmed at this rapidly growing
hazard that societies have been formed, including government
agencies. On January 1st, eleven areas were designated National Parks,
and it is intended to increase their number, Rondane, Pasvik, and
Borgefjell are the most famous. Pasvik, just South of Kirkenes, is
unique, for being close to the Soviet Union, it possesses the Western
extremity of the taiga (coniferous forest) which stretches for
thousands of miles across Siberia and Northern Russia.

And to all those finde idealists who are striving hard to preserve the
splendour of Norway's Nature, I wish them every success. For it is
not only our generation which will benefit, but many generations to come.

THE CLIMATE

If much of Norway was in Alaska, Northern Canada, or Siberia, the land would be in the region of perma-frost. But, thanks to the warming influence of the Gulf Stream, the temperatures are much higher than other lands in similar latitudes. This warm current keeps the harbours open throughout the year, while, the Swedish and Finnish ports on the Gulf of Bothnia are often ice bound for a considerable period.

In the East the climate changes between Summer and Winter are more marked, Oslo being much colder than Bergen in Winter, and warmer in Summer. The Eastern valleys are much drier, Oslo has about 42 cm (20 inches) of rain annually, Bergen about 126 cm (82 in)

Oslo is just as cold as Trornso, almost 1,000 miles further North, in January, being a long way from the open sea, while the Finnmark region, in the extreme North, and Roros, in the East, have 230—245 days each year with temperatures below freezing. Bergen situated latitude 60 degrees North, is only 2 degrees cooler than Princetown on Dartmoor, 50 degrees N. (3 and 1 degree C. resp. 34 and 37 degrees F).

POPULATION

The present population of Norway is almost 4 million, and when one compares it to that of Great Britain, with about 55 million on the same land area, the difference is extremely great. Roughly 48% live in rural districts, and about 52% in towns and built up areas.

Most of the people are members of the Nordic Race, fair, tall and long-skulled people, with blue eyes. On the West and South coasts the inhabitants are of mixed stock, Alpine and Nordic, there are also people of Baltic origin, whose ancestors emigrated from Finland, in the Southern forests and far North. In Northern Norway, the latter group (kvener) has maintained it's distinctive characteristics.

In the North too, the Lapps, who number some 20 thousand have a completely different language and culture from the Norwegians. They have lived there since prehistoric days, living chiefly by hunting, reindeer herding, and fishing, and have dark hair and eyes with a rather short and stocky stature.

MAIN CITIES.

Oslo, Norway's capital, has a population of nearly 500,000 and an area of 175 sq. miles, 60% of this being wooded. It has the unique position of not only being Norway's leading industrial, commercial, and shipping town, but having splendid natural surroundings. Only a few minutes drive from the bustling town centre can take you to the densely wooded slopes of the Holmenkollen mountain, World-famed for it's Winter sports, or a sun-blessed beach on the side of the blue Oslo-fjord. It is truly remarkable that so much beauty can be found so near the factories, docks, and workshops which do so much to help the progress of the Norwegian people.

Bergen, Norway's second largest city, with over 200,000 inhabitants, is a very old shipping, trading, and industrial centre. It has much of historical and cultural importance, and holds annually an International Summer Festival of Music. The multitude of quaint old buildings, nestling below the steep hills, the renown Hanseatic wooden houses on the waterfront, built when the Dutch and Germans traded extensively with Norway, and the splendour of the nearby fjords and mountains, make Bergen an ideal touring centre. And one can never forget the hospitality of the Bergen citizens, their zest for living, and spontaneous humour and good-will.

Trondheim, is about the same size as Bergen, and for many years was the capital of Norway. It is also an important trading, industrial and shipping centre., and the ancient Nidaros cathedral is the highest in Northern Europe.

This town too has a special charm of it's own, as I discovered one morning

86

after returning from a long journey to Arctic Norway and Swedish Lapland. The brightly painted houses, cobbled street, flower market, and magnificent railway station, make each journey more than worthwhile. And the inhabitants are friendly, jovial, and extremely reliable.

Stavanger, 90,000 population, is one of the oldest towns in Norway, and it's cathedral dates back to 1125. Today it is Norway's biggest ship-building port, and carries on fish-canning on a huge scale, even having a technical school specialising on the fin art of fish canning.

Kristiansand, population 63,000, is the 'capital' of the South Coast and is well-known for trade and shipping. An ideal centre to start a highly enjoyable holiday in Norway the sublime.

Drammen, with 60,000 people, is the administrative centre of the Buskerud county, and next to Oslo and Sarpsborg, is Norway's third largest timber exporter.

Skien, with 50 thousand people, is the trade centre of Telemark, and the birthplace of Henrik Ibsen, the famous poet and playwright.

Alesund, with a population of 45,000 is the land's most important fishing centre and is blessed with truly magnificent surroundings. Nearby is the Geiranger Fjord, the lofty Sunnmore Alps, Andalsnes and the scenic Romsdal Peak and Trolltindene mountains. The grandeur of the nature is inspiring and invigorating.

Tromso, with roughly 40,000 inhabitants, covers a bigger area than any other town in Norway. It is the seat of the World's most Northern university, which has now been recently established.

Norway has a merchant navy of 21 million tons, and only Liberia, Japan, and Great Britain have a larger shipping capacity. This is about 7 per cent of the total World Shipping, and in every port in East and West the Norwegian flag waves gaily under a bright sky.

Fishing and forestry play a vital part in the prosperity of the Norwegians as does the Electro-metallurgical and Electro-chemical industries. Norsk-Hydro is today the largest exporter of nitrogen in Europe.

Hydro-electric power is of great importance and supplies a cheap and plentiful source of power to industry, some of it is exported, mainly to Sweden and Finland.

FINLAND

Finland after Iceland is the most Northern land in the World, and about a third of her total length is situated North of the Arctic Circle. With a population just under 5 million, and a land area of 130 thousand sq miles (337,000 sq. kilometers). the density of population is fairly sparse most of the people live in the South and near the Western coast.

In other words, Finland has a population roughly half that of greater London.

The land is rather low, but it not of the flat, lowland type, the rocky hillocks, valleys, and ridges give the landscape a fascinating character of it's own. In the North the high hills are known as 'Tunturi' their lower slopes are generally covered with spruce and birch forests, and the tops only give stunted growth of mosses and grass. The highest mountain, Haltiatunturi, 4,354 ft. (1,328 meters) is near the Norwegian frontier, and this region is becoming increasingly popular for Winter sports.

Finland has about 60,000 lakes, which comprise 9% of the total area. Saimaa has a surface area of 1,700 miles (4,400 sq. kilometers) followed by Paijanne and Inari. These lakes form a highly useful means of transport, the floating of timber, and recreation, and a leisurely trip by steamer is something not to be missed.

The climate is somewhat more severe than Norway or Southern Sweden, being more remote from the warming influence of the Gulf Stream and being closer to the Soviet Union. But the Summers are delightfully warm, I remember experiencing a heat wave, with temperatures well into the eighties (about 26 to 28 C) while being in Kuusamo, just South of the Arctic Circle.

Summer, with a mean temperature of 50f. (10 C) lasts for 110 to 122 days in the South, and 50 to 85 days in the North. The land is snow-bound for about 5 months in the south and 7 months in the North. A schoolteacher told me one year at Rovaniemi, just South of the Arctic Circle, the snow came in early September, and stayed until the middle of May. But during the brief Summers in Northern Finland, the almost perpetual daylight and bright sunshine makes agriculture possible right up to the Arctic Circle.

LANGUAGE.

Racially the Finns are mixed, the main stocks derive from the East Baltic and Nordic races. Finns are generally of light complexion, having fair hair and blue eyes. The language is closely related to Hungarian and Estonian and belongs to the Finno-Ugrian family. Many of the Finns speak Swedish, and in towns such as Vaasa and Parainen on the coastal strip, Swedish is the spoken tongue. About 7% speak Swedish. The Lapps. who live in the Far North, and number some 2,000 also speak their own language, Lappish.

INDUSTRY

Finland has over 70% of her land area under forests, and only the Soviet Union and Sweden are the European lands which have even larger resources. To the average Finn, the forest it the main source of livelihood, both in the home and export market. Sawn timber, plywood, chemical pulp, paperboard, and newsprint prove valuable items of export, the forest means to the Finn what the sea is to a Norwegian, farming to a Dane, or steel to a Swede.

Textiles also form an important export to many European lands, machinery to a lesser degree, and shipbuilding. The Finns construct some of the finest ships in the World, especially icebreakers, which are eagerly sought after by the Russians, owing to their strength and tenacity.

The Finns are highly educated and probably read far more books per person than any other nation. Women have equal rights to men, and often become capable doctors, lawyers, and technicians. The Finns have some of the World's finest architects, full of initiative and imagination, and build houses which are light, practical, warm and ultra-modern.

Most of the forests are privately owned, and the men generally work in nearby towns to ensure a reliable livelihood. As in most other lands, there has been a drift of population from the farms to the factories, before the war most of the people lived on the land, now just as many are working in the towns.

TOWNS.

The principal towns are, Helsinki, the capital, with over ½ million inhabitants, followed by Tampere, 160,000 and Turku, 150,000. These are followed by Lahti, 90,000 Oulu, 85,000, Pori, 75,000 Jyvaskyla, 60,000, and Kuopio, 57,000.

ICELAND

Iceland, with an area of 103,000 sq. kilometers (40,000 sq. miles) is the second largest island in Europe. It is a land of great contrasts, with long, green valleys stretching inland from the rugged coast, high plateaus with snow-capped peaks, lava formations, rushing rivers, high waterfalls, geysers, and still active vulcanoes.

This is the land of far horizons, crystal-clear air, and long, warm Summer days with bright sunshine and nights where the glow of a superb sunset with the first signs of another dawn. During the long Winter nights the sky is often lit by the Northern Lights, Aurora Borealis, a truly fantastic display of Nature's radiant power.

Iceland is one of the most renown lands for vulkanoes, the most recent eruptions being from Hekla, Askja and Surtsey. And of far great importance for the hardy and industrious Islanders, the multitude of hot springs and geysers. They are of vital means of heating of homes and greenhouses, even grapes and oranges can be grown under glass. And the capital, Reykjavik, is heated by several geysers, schools, libraries and other facilities are pleasantly warm even in the middle of an icy Winter day.

The land has an ocean climate, and the winds from the North Atlantic tempered by the warming influence of the Gulf Stream keeps the ports icefree throughout the year. Places much farther South in Canada and the Soviet Union are in the perma-frost region, where the sub-soil is frozen even in the middle of the Summer. Reykjavik has an average mean temperature of 4 degrees C.(about 39 degrees F.) and in July the average temperature is 11 degrees C. (52 F.). But often rapid temperature changes take place, as cold winds suddenly blow from the Arctic.

A great setback to progress is the almost complete lack of natural resources, there are no mineral reserves or coal seams, and only fishing and sheep rearing give the land valuable export markets. Electric power from the rivers is the chief source of power for the population of just over 200,000 inhabitants.

Iceland was uninhabited until the Vikings came from Norway over a thousand years ago. Ingolf Arnason founded the Icelandic Nation at the end of the 9th century, the approx. year was 874. These hardy, courageous Vikings did not stop merely in Iceland, in 982 Greenland was discovered from Iceland, and from Greenland Leifur Eriksson sailed westwards and discovered North America in 1,000 A.D. The majority of the population is of Norwegian origin, and also a small minority came from the British Isles. The language is the oldest still used in Europe, as it was spoken throughout the Scandinavian lands when Iceland was discovered. This language was the foundation of the old Icelandic literature of the 12th and 13th century.

There is no nation in Europe which is so sparsely inhabited, and even the capital, Rejkjavik, has only 80,000 inhabitants which is quite small by British standards. About 80% live in towns and large villages on the coast, as the interior is generally too barren to support much human inhabitation. Industry is carried on by 25% of the people, agriculture 13%, trade and communications 24%, building 13%, public services 19%, and fishing 6%. The latter is the most important for the export trade and foreign currency.

Today, the export of fish is as vital to Iceland as the export of timber products is for Finland, and 90% of the export consists of fish and fish products.

At the turn of the century about 73% of the population was engaged in agriculture, and now it is only 13%. More and more people are engaged in industry and fishing, and yet the agricultural production has not been minimised. Modern machinery and improved methods have made it possible for Iceland to develop her land use. A small amount of frozen mutton is exported, and Iceland is self-supporting for meat, milk, butter, and cheese.

Iceland is completely different to Sweden and Finland as regards forest areas. When the Vikings first discovered Iceland, it was thickly forested, but rapid exploitation of the woods and intensive grazing by cattle soon depleted her forests. Finland has 70% under forests, Sweden about 54%, and Iceland only 1%. Today trees are being successfully planted and the time will surely come when well cared-for forests will yield productive timber.

It is almost impossible to grow barley, wheat, and oats, as the Summers are much cooler and damper than in the Scandinavian lands. So most of the fodder for cattle has to be imported, yet the yields of hay and grass is extremely high.

Fifty years ago only 3% of the population was occupied with industry, today it is 25%. The majority of factory workers help with fish preserving and canning, while others are busy with textiles, net-making shipwharves, machine shops, and building.

Hydro-electric power from the rivers is of great use for a cement and fertiliser factory, and a large, new aluminium plant to the South of the Hafnarfjord.

Owing to it's isolated position Iceland has a larger foreign trade than any other land in relation to it's population. Iceland produces a large quantity of relatively few products, but used small amounts of many products.

Iceland has no railway network, as the population is small and the terrain too mountanous and unproductive. Bus, boat, and air transport connect the various towns and villages, usually situated near the coast. During the last 15 years internal air routes have rapidly developed. There are about 100 airports served by 17 planes. And even the remotest farm is served by an efficient telephone network and the majority of families have a television.

Social help to families, old, and sick people is one of the finest in the World, and is very similar to that of the other Northern lands. Even 1,000 years ago, in the age of the ancient Sagas and the first Viking settlers, Farmers were responsible tó help their neighbours with damage caused by fires and other catastrophies. This spirit of self-sacrifice and determination has made these small nations great in humanitarian ethics.

The young citizens of Iceland have excellent prospects of having a good education. Elementary education is offered to all students from the age of 7 to 15. Later, if they so wish, education can be continued at technical colleges and art schools. The Icelandic University at Reykjavik gives young people with ability the chance to become engineers, jurists, doctors, and teachers.

The literature is rich in it's variety and high level of cultural development, and is as old as the history of this 'Land of Sagas'. All children have the opportunity of learning about their land's literature from an early age.

Iceland is unique in possessing the oldest parliament in the World, The Altinget was founded in 930, and it's thousand years anniversary was celebrated in 1930, and the village of Tingvellir, about 50 kilometers from Reykjavik. Altinget consists of a higher and lower house, there are 60 elected members, and their period of office lasts 4 years.

ICELANDS LONG STRUGGLE FOR FREEDOM AND INDEPENDENCE.

After many internal struggles Iceland was under the Norwegian jurisdiction from the 13th century, and later it was Denmark which decided Iceland's destiny. In 1918, Iceland became self-governing, although still united to Denmark. Finally, in 1944, Iceland achieved complete self-determination.

The two World Wars had a great influence on the rapid development of Iceland. Right up until the end of the 19th century the hard-working people of farmers and fishermen lived under extremely poor and primitive conditions. About 90% of the population lived under extremely poor and primitive conditions. About 90% of the population lived in houses made of turf, and there were no roads, no harbours, no hospitals, and schools were few and far between.

In the last 60 years huge steps have been made in the social progress especially during and after the second World War.

There is much co-operation with the other four Scandinavian lands and World wide interest in international and European organisation. And it is by hard work, good-will, and determination that the people of Iceland have enriched their own lives and the fortunate visitor who is made welcome in their inspiring land of wide horizons and magnificent natural scenery.

SWEDEN

A large and greatly diversified natural environment has shaped the
Swedish people and society of today. Endless miles of coniferous
forests extend over nearly all the land, from the rugged hills of
Smaland in the South, to the fells of Lapland in the remove North.
The Central plains support well kept farms which are generally large,
while in the extreme South- West, in the province of Skane, the people
and flat landscape are very similar to Denmark. Thousands of lakes
dot the valleys throughout the vast expanse of land, and mighty rivers
flow into the Baltic and Gulf of Bothnia, carrying power to the hydro-
electric stations, and timber to the hungry sawmills situated near their
wide estuaries.

In many aspects Sweden resembles Canada, with farming in the extreme
South, forestry and mining further North, and huge areas of sub-Arctic
wastes in the Arctic Regions.

Situated between 55 degrees North (just South of Edinburgh) and 69
degrees N. (well North of Iceland) there is a tremendous comparison
between the climate and way of life between North and South. With
it's 174,000 sq. miles (450,000 sq. kilometers) it has almost twice
the land area of the United Kingdom, and the population is just over
8 million.

The highest mountains are in the North, near the Norwegian frontier,
the Kebnekaise, nearly 7,000 ft. followed by the Sarekjakko and
Sulitelma, almost as high.

Less than 100 years ago agriculture was the predominant element, and
even as late as 1,900 some 90 per cent of the people lived in their
red wooden cottages which even today give the rolling landscape, of
hills, woods, glittering lakes, and smiling meadows, under a clear blue
sky dotted with wisps of cloud, a special charm of it's own.

Agriculture did not bring high earnings, poverty was rife which led to mass emigration to the United States and Canada.

But the mountains and remote forests contained vast natural resources, and in due course steel, wood, and paper formed the basis of rapid industrial development which had already taken place in more advanced European lands about 80 to 100 year earlier.

Sweden began to export on an ever-increasing scale iron-ore of extremely high quality to many European lands, together with wood products of various kinds.

The Swedish engineering products became renowned for their high reliability and endurance, and in the mining districts a multitude of industries flourished. Initiative and hard-work helped many energetic Swedes to form small metalworking companies all over the country, most of them being under 50 years since being founded.

Textile concerns had a long and tedious struggle against foreign competition, yet now able able to export about 20 per cent of their products.

The shipbuilding industry is of vital importance, and today Sweden has now surpassed England and Germany in ship production, only that industrial giant Japan exceeds Sweden in the number of ships being built. Strong but sensible trade unions, fair-play and teamwork between employee and employers have made this possible.

Agriculture is no longer of special importance, and each day that passes brings a few abandoned farmsteads in it's rather sad wake. But many of the remaining farms become bigger, resourceful, and highly efficient.

A delightful and friendly balance is maintained between a Socialist Government and the brains and genius of private enterprise. Many concerns are State-owned, such as the State Railways, National Telecommunications, a government-owned State Bank, and Post Office Savings Bank. Otherwise all commercial and industrial enterprises are privately owned.

There is a tremendous spirit of co-operation between the trade unions and the government and private enterprise, so that both sides greatly benefit and make progress in a splendid manner.

A strong love of Peace, a policy of strict neutrality, help and sincere understanding to less fortunate lands, has been inspired by those worthy individuals and idealists who enrich and ennoble the lives of their fellow-men.

And so it is time to leave you with a multitude of pleasant and happy thoughts of these splendid Northern lands and their sturdy and hospitable peoples. One's thoughts wander from the snow capped mountains to the fjords and farmlands, from the remote villages to the ultra-modern capitals and busy factories and workshops.

But above all, one is inspired with the Spirit of the People. With their honest toil, often against extreme climatic conditions, they have together brought Peace, Prosperity, and Progress to these Nordic lands.

And it is the Spirit of these People which has forged the true Spirit of the Brotherhood of Mankind and Progressive Idealism.

MYRDAL STATION. A SPLENDID SETTING IN NORWAY THE SUBLIME

ARCTIC
CIRCLE

NARVIK

KIRUNA

ROVANIEMI

TRONDHEIM

SWEDEN

KAJAANI

ANDALSNES

FINLAND

NORWAY

TAMPERE

BERGEN

OSLO

KARLSTAD

AREMDAL

STOCKHOLM

HELSINKI

GÖTEBORG

DENMARK

USSR

COPENHAGEN

FASCINATING FINLAND, LAND OF FORESTS AND LAKES BECKONS.!!

For several years I had longed to visit Finland, the land of lakes and forests, and hard working, hospitable people had always attracted me. September seemed the most favourable time to travel, for my work in Sweden for the Summer had been finished, and the days were still quite warm and sunny. I felt a thrill of excitement and adventure as I sailed from Stockholm late one evening, and saw the stately buildings of this lovely capital slowly disappear as the open sea was reached. A multitude of islands was passed, many of them were used as the Summer homes of the city dwellers, others were fishing hamlets. How peaceful the log cabins looked by the rocky shores of the thickly wooded islands, and as the twilight slowly descended, their bright lights were reflected on the calm waters of the Baltic.

Overhead the sky was clear, with countless stars twinkling brightly and I seemed to live in a strange, silent world. I felt so completely free, and my heart and soul were at joyous peace with the world and universe.!! I found it almost impossible to sleep that night and spent half the time in conversation with Finnish and Swedish passengers. As the faint streaks of dawn slowly strengthened, the whole sky turned a deep crimson over the calm sea and skerries off the Finish coast.

On arrival in Turku, I immediately took a brisk walk, breathing in the clear crisp air. Turku is Finland's oldest city, and near the centre still retains many of its low timbered houses, narrow streets, and rather cramped shops and buildings of merchants.

I enjoyed walking in these old fashioned, mellowed surroundings, so completely different to the hectic world of today. I took a tram to explore more of this former capital, it was smaller and less luxuriant than its Swedish counterpart in Stockholm, but everywhere I saw parks which were a delight to any gardener. Many of the streets were flanked by avenues of graceful birch trees. I have seen these birches everywhere in Finland, from the Soviet frontier in the east to Rovaniemi in the far north. Their barks gleamed like shafts of silver in the rays of the bright sunshine, their simplicity and fascination had much in common with the Finnish citizens. Formerly Swedish trade and influence dominated, and the ancient castle and cathedral were built under their administration. Today English and Swedish are the chief languages taught, and in some of the smaller towns on the west and south coasts, Swedish in the dominant language.

Often I came across women working on building sites, for Finland is far more eastern in her ways than Sweden, but she is at the same time truly democratic, for her people have integrity, idealism, and the will to work and make progress. The Finnish women have the opportunity to

99

receive a thorough education, and often become skilled doctors, engineers, and architects. Not so long ago, Finland suffered poverty and unemployment on a vast scale, but thanks to work and determination things have rapidly improved. She a is strong believer in strict neutrality, and so has helped to build a bridge of peace and goodwill between east and west.

In Turku I first experienced the spontaneous hospitality which I later found to be so typical of the Finns. A business-man who I had met on the boat offered me a lift in his car to Helsinki. It was not long before we were amongst forests, lakes, and a landscape with gently undulating hills and sparkling streams shining brightly in the bright Autumn sunshine. As Helsinki was approached we crossed over several high bridges, and their graceful design blended with the inlets, islands, and woods which surrounded the city. As the first suburbs of the city passed by, I noticed how modern and imaginative their architecture was, simple, clear cut, and modern, a joy for all to behold.!!

During the past fifteen years probably no nation has made such a great contribution to modern architecture as Finland has. This can be attributed to the high standard of workmanship and ability to improve its technique in many aspects. If we have time to visit the Pensions Building, and other nearby buildings, we immediately find out how true this is. New talent is found, not merely by examinations, but putting initiative and imagination into practice.!! Unfortunately in Helsinki, as in most other cities, devastating fires have destroyed most buildings of historical importance. In Finland approximately seventy churches date back to the middle ages, of which Turku Cathedral is the largest. Helsinki was almost completely destroyed by fire in 1808. The population is about half a million, but the wide streets keep the traffic congestion at a minimum And the green parks and gardens give both pleasure and relaxation for both office and factory workers, there are several theatres, including Finland's National Theatre. The garden city of Tapiola is one of the finest in Europe, and is not far from the city centre, many nations can learn much from a visit here. Helsinki has built a simple national monument to Runeberg, Finland's national poet.

At the granite central railway station I bought a single ticket to Porvoo, a quite idyllic town of old-world charm which has hardly changed. I dozed off for some time during the short journey, but was wide awake when the train pulled into the small railway station. As I walked along a road leading upwards through the town, I relaxed amongst the old wooden buildings which helped to retain the right atmosphere for poets and artists. I found a small cafe, and drinking strong coffee and cake enjoyed watching the people stroll through the narrow cobbled streets.

The sun was low in the western sky as I thumbed a lift on a lorry driven by a jovial driver, the road was lonely and poorly paved. As the sun set below the purple horizon, its red glow lit up the deep red bark of the lofty pine trees, the neatly stacked piles of hay, and the rustic wooden fences.

As the straggling town of Lovissa was reached I decided to stop for the night. A small mobile fair had encamped here, and some of the Finnish music, played over a blaring loudspeaker, sounded quite eastern, contrasting so strongly to the quietness of the surrounding forests. Only a few days ago the Don Cossacks and their superb horses had been performing. I could visualise them so clearly, sweeping across the Russian Steppes, their hooves pounding on the firm soil. Don Cossacks, the very word brought excitement.

A passer-by indicated the road to the nearby youth hostel, it was about a mile distant, reached by a winding road through the forest. As the distant noise of the town slowly became fainter, I had never experienced such complete silence.!! The tall pine trees stood up like silent sentinels, against a sky full of stars which shone with an unusual brilliance. Only a day ago I had been in the heart of Stockholm, yet here civilisation seemed so distant and too remote to comprehend. Again and again I looked at the bright northern sky.

I reached the farm which was in a clearing in the forest and the farmer and his wife bid me welcome. They had a sweet little daughter, a five year old with flaxen hair, and an open, happy face. How I loved watching her joyful expression when I gave her some chocolate. I was the only traveller staying there, and in no time I was fast asleep, what luxury it was to really be able to sleep so well and so long.!!

Waking early, I looked out into the forest clearing, and much to my amazement, found the ground was glistening with the first Autumn frost. The nearest supply of water was from a pump in the farm-courtyard, so carrying a bucket, I warmed some of it on a stove and had a thorough wash. I felt so energetic, that I did not even stop for breakfast, and saying Goodbye, thanked the farming couple for their hospitality. With the song of the open road in my soul, I headed at full spead for the coastal road. After reaching Lovissa I came to a halt by an old wooden bridge and basking in the already warm sunshine, watched the agile fishes dart to and fro. I almost found time for day dreaming, how many people had crossed this bridge, Finns, Russians, Germans, and Swedes, what a multitude of tales it could relate, of war and peace, hope and love.!!

After waiting for about half an hour, a large taxi suddenly came to a grinding halt, leaving a cloud of dust in its wake. Out stepped the driver, a remarkable specimen of vitality and radiant health, tall, muscular and alert. He looked like a Greek statue, and being able to speak fluent Swedish, made our conversation highly interesting. Kotka, a large town by Finnish standards, was quickly reached. A hundred years ago Kotka was a mere fishing village, but is now the most important export town and specialises in shipping paper, timber, wood pulp, and other forest products. More plywood passes through this port than any other in the world, and each year 4,000 ships from all corners of the earth load their valuable cargoes. I walked through the docks and chatted to some of the cheerful dockers. I would have even liked to have worked here, but time was short.!

Above Kotka are situated the rushing falls of Langinkoski, with the fishing cabin of the Imperial Czar. Once it belonged to Czar Alexander III and Dagmar, his Danish wife. The aroma of fresh coffee wafted in my nostrils, so I was soon inside a small snack-bar, which seemed so warm in comparison to the cold east wind outside. It was a long, rather strenuous walk to the outskirts of the town, and after a few minutes I was joined by a Finnish sailor who was going home on leave. But we soon parted company, as he carried a bottle of cheap Vodka, and from time to time would stop to have a sip.

An old shaky car stopped, and the driver gave me a short lift, and took me to his small farmstead. He worked most of the time in the docks, many farmers in Finland work a considerable part of their available time in industry in order to earn a reasonable living. His wife was delightfully happy so I felt completely at home with them. I drank strong, sweet coffee and partook of freshly made homely food. He was a Communist and had two sons who worked on the Volga Don canal. I refused to join them in drinking some alcohol, and thanking them, headed on. The farmer was thoughtful enough to stop a passing timber lorry and so I was taken to Hamina, a small but lively town not far from the Russian frontier.

With its low wooden houses, roughly paved streets, and Russian Orthodox Church topped by onion-shaped copulas, the town had a distinctly Eastern atmosphere. While waiting for a lift, I watched a railway engine shunting, it used timber as a source of power, such engines are very uncommon in Europe today. After a long wait, I was given a lift, it seemed strange to see the huge, lonely forests, and a few villages in forest clearings. On and on we sped, the forest seemed unending, until as twilight descended we reached Lappeenranta, a small town on the edge of Lake Saimaa. Here I drank some coffee as I felt stiff and tired after the long trip, before boarding a waiting bus. Some of the younger passengers tried to join in conversation, but with my scanty knowledge of Finnish, this was almost impossible.

On arrival at Imatra it had become dark and rather cold, so I lost no time in looking for a place to stay the night. But nowhere could I find accommodation, how lost and forlorn I felt, even my usual good humour seemed to vanish. At the biggest hotel I pleaded with the receptionist, and after a patient wait, he managed to put me up in a bed in the bathroom.! It was hot and stuffy, the heat was full on, and there was no window for ventilation. Almost like a Finnish sauna bath, I cooly remarked with a wide grin. After breakfast I was able to see something of the small industrialised town. The Imatrakoski rapids are now dammed tô provide the largest hrdro-electric power station in Finland with its requirements. Imatra has some of the largest paper and cellulose mills in the World. The Church of Three Crosses designed by Alvar Aalto, is a masterpiece of straight pure lines full of brightness from quietly concealed windows.

Still heading north, I continued on my journey past countless blue lakes amongst the thick pine forests. At Simpele, the most eastern point on my route, the road was a mere hundred yards from the Soviet Union, but the frontier was apparently deserted.

It was a long time before I had a fresh lift near Simpele, as the traffic was scarce, but I quite enjoyed waiting in the bright sunshine. The road was winding, dusty and narrow, and often ran close to the side of Lake Saimaa, its waters gleaming in the afternoon sun, now quite low in the sky. At Punkaharju, a long ridge of narrow land crossing Lake Saimaa, I found the beauty and peacefulness very inspiring, it was so quiet I could almost hear nature speak. The eastern province of Karelia is perhaps the lovliest region of Finland, and together with Lapland, is my favourite region. The car drove past Hotel Finlandia, this is a well-known hotel and extremely popular.

The very name brought the sound of Sibelius to my imagination. How much joy this gifted composer had given to people of all nationalities, apart from the citizens of his own beloved country. Already in his boyhood days he would wander in the lonely woods with his violin, in dedicated appreciation to the birds, the forest animals, and the slender silver birches. His music, both strong and tender, full of intense feeling and emotion, is immortal and unchanged in its simplicity, strength, and beauty. In all he left a legacy of over two hundred works of music, many complete masterpieces, a worthy tribute to the hardy, creative Finnish people.

Even as a youth, while farming in Gloucestershire, I became very fond of his music. As I looked at the nearby rolling hills of the Forest of Dean, I could clearly visualise the deep blue lakes, the pine forests, and snow falling quietly on isolated farmsteads in the depth of winter. I can still hear "Valse Triste" and "Kullerva" ringing clearly in my ears. And as with the majority of poets and highly talented musicians, life to him was a challenge, and a thing of beauty, to be appreciated fully by work, spirit, and determination. One late night, a sudden impluse influenced him to drive from Helsinki to his home at the village of Kerava, and this inspired his work "Night Ride to Sunrise". The rural surroundings and the rythmic movement of the horse and carriage gave him a great impulse to compose, and one can clearly hear the beating of the horses hooves, the crisp rustle of upturned leaves, and the song of the birds, increasing as the forest awakes to a new day.!! And the gradual, delicate changes of colour of the clear sky as a glorious day dawns.

By late afternoon I arrived at my final destination, the small town of Savonlinna, situated by the lakeside, quite unhurried and only little changed by modern progress, apart from a few scattered blocks of flats. A few pleasure boats made the best of few days left before Autumn set in, and well kept gardens blended with the background of old rustic homes. I appreciated the relaxed friendly atmosphere of this remote town.

At a small hotel run by the Salvation Army, I found a room for the night. I was just in time to watch a splendid sunset, the tall pines stood silent over the calm waters, which reflected the brightness of the

103

crimson sky. It was a delightful setting to a long, strenuous, and fascinating journey, and I felt so grateful to being able to see such varied beautiful landscapes. And I had the joyous gratitude towards the Finnish people, with their open-hearted hospitality and spontaneous help and good humoured outlook on Life.!!

One of the joys of travelling by train in Scandinavia in Summer is the opportunity to see myriads of wild flowers.

In June and July the mauve Wood Cranesbill clothes many banks, a little later there are stretches of carmine Rosebay Willow Herb. Throughout the Summer the clear blue Harebells (the Bluebells of Scotland) abound everywhere. In some areas, including Myrdal and Upsete, the tall, purple Monkshood flourishes.

As well as the many common species, a number of rarer ones are to be found on or near the stations. Gentians bloom near one main line junction and the halt at Kjosfossen is a paradise for keen botanists. Among the mountain flowers, Saussurea, Grass of Parnassus, Starry Saxifrage, the orange form of Yellow Saxifrage, Mountain Queen and Melancholy Thistle are just a few that can be seen from a train in Western Norway.

In areas near the tree-line the dark green ground cover, in Summer, is Dwarf Birch and this becomes a rich red in Autumn. The low grey-green growth is Willow. Above the tree-line in places Reindeer Moss colours the rocks sage-green.

As Autumn approaches, the many varieties of berries add colour to the landscape. Clusters of scarlet berries festoon the northern Elder and the fruits of the Rowan become a glowing shade of vermillion, while low on the ground are red Cowberries and Cranberries and black Bearberries, Bilberries and Crowberries. The legendary Cloudberry (Molte in Norwegian) is difficult to find but it does fruit earlier in different places in the mountains.

From the high mountains to the sheltered valleys, Autumn brings a harvest of beauty and colour.

THE JOY OF TRAIN TRAVEL
SOME USEFUL HINTS AND ADVICE

Travelling by train in Scandinavia is safe, reliable, comfortable, and last but not least, a highly enjoyable form of relaxing travel to explore these fascinating Northern lands.

You can reach with ease hundreds of large and smaller towns and scenic resorts at your leisure, still fresh and relaxed, and ready to enjoy yet another day. And, in the chief railway stations, such as Stockholm, Helsinki, Oslo, and Copenhagen, you will find most helpful services, such as food, money exchange, hotel and room advice to suit all pockets and tastes, and very useful tourist information.

I strongly recommend you to book and carefully plan your travel itinerary a long time ahead, at least several months ahead, in order to achieve maximum enjoyment, carefree relaxation, and knowledge of local customs. By doing so you will gain far more knowledge of these scenic lands and so save valuable time and inconvenience while on vacation.

The busiest month is July, as the Scandinavians and other Europeans generally take their Summer holidays at this rather hectic time. So, where possible, mid-May, June, late August, and September are the best months, those who can come in April can enjoy blue skies, sun, and snow, and in September the splendour of Autumn colours in the high mountains must be seen to be believed.

Once you have decided where to go, it will be quite easy to write for brochures about the towns and areas which are of greatest interest. Furthermore, you may wish to make a certain town as a base for making easy day trips, e.g. Oslo, Trondheim, Bergen, Voss, Ulvik, Stockholm, Helsinki, so you could decide exactly where to stay. In this case, you might like to use not only one, but perhaps two, three, or even four towns as your bases.

Perhaps this is rather prejudiced, but the west of Norway is my favourite area, for here one finds, in more than abundance, fjords, forests, rivers, lakes, and mountains in ever-changing grandeur and moods. The splendour of nature blends with human kindness in no uncertain manner. Here too is to be found a large variety of hotels, friendly guest houses, motels, and Summer chalets.

For splendid views, try the Flam area, where the Fretheim hotel and Heimly pension bid you welcome. And for a truly relaxed holiday by the shores of the sheltered Hardanger fjord I suggest the comfort of the Brakanes hotel, where Per Hide and his charming wife bid you

105

welcome. And Bjorn and Hanna Hjaltnes, who own the delightful Ulvik hotel are well known in many lands for their warm hospitality and first-class cuisine.

If you have time, the well-known Stalheim hotel can be easily reached by a regular bus service, in just under an hour from Voss railway station. Lunchtime is an ideal time to arrive, for their famous open-table "Smargasbord" needs time to enjoy to the fullest. In former times Stalheim was an inn, here since 1647 it was used by the "pony-express" when the mail was carried on horseback, and this spot was ideal for changing the horses and riders. The hotel also possesses a museum of a wonderful variety of farm houses and relics of great historical interest. And from the terrace of the hotel is a heavenly view over the Brekke, Jordal and Naro valleys, the Sivle and Stalheim waterfalls, and the conical peak of Mt. Jordal.

Near most stations there are generally large hotels, whilst the smaller pensions and guest houses are highly attractive, and their prices are modest too. Often, while staying with a family, one gains added and intimate knowledge of the friendly, honest, and hospitable Northern peoples, and both for young and old, the youth hostels are of a high standard as regards helpful and friendly advice, good, plain cooking, and light, clean rooms.

And, meeting the people is the best and happiest way of getting to know more of these progressive and democratic lands.

Throughout the Nordic lands are a large variety of youth hostels affording accommodation to tourists at a moderate price, regardless of age or nationality. Some have rooms especially for families, most have hot and cold showers and many of the smaller ones, such as the hostel at Andalsnes, is on a farm. Here one can wake up in the morning and hear the sound of waterfalls and the dawn chorus of birds. The hostels in Geilo and Trondheim can find enough room for over 200 people, whilst Haraldsheim hostel in Oslo is almost as busy as a railway station. The Voss hostel is situated on the edge of Lake Vossevangen and is ultra-modern, almost like a luxury hotel, with hot showers and toilet for every room. And seldom can one find a view which can compare with that from the wide windows of Montana youth hostel. In the evenings one can enjoy many a splendid sunset, and watch the fairyland of lights brightly glittering from the city of Bergen. At one hostel on a farm near Lovissa I had to pump water from the courtyard well on a cold and frosty morning, but how I enjoyed it.

SCENIC ROUTES OF OUTSTANDING BEAUTY

Everywhere one turns in Scandinavia one is surrounded by natural beauty. Denmark has gently rolling hills, fertile farmsteads, quiet beech woods, ancient buildings and castles, busy modern towns, and old-world villages little changed by time.

106

Finland has thousands of tranquil blue lakes, vast pine forests, sun-drenched beaches, and homes and public buildings of outstanding architectural achievement. To the north the vast wilderness of Finnish Lapland still retains something of the old pioneer spirit. Here roam bear and lynx, and other animals also protected by law. Further to the east, towns such as Imatra, with its rapids, and Savonlinna, with a medieval castle, are well worth a visit. Lake Saimaa and Lake Paijanne offer scenic boat trips and the mountains near the Norwegian border are ideal for winter sports.

Sweden has a great variety of natural scenery stretching from the fertile plains of Skane to the huge forests of Varmland and Norrland, and the Arctic fells near Abisko and Kiruna. Bohuslan is one of my favourite provinces, where the windswept rugged coastline gives way to sheltered valleys and steep hills covered with heather, birch and pine woods. Then there is Varmland, renowned for its beauty, friendly people, and for its poets and writers such as Selma Lagerlof and Gustaf Froding. Stockholm, the Venice of the North, Gothenburg, and many other towns retain much of historical and cultural interest. From the old university towns of Lund and Uppsala one can make wonderful day excursions. The lakeside resorts of Rattvik and Mora in Dalarna still retain old customs and traditions.

NORWAY THE SUBLIME

Norway is still my favourite land, possessing so many great contrasts of scenic beauty, stretching from the warm, smiling valleys and wooded hills of the south, the low farming land and huge forests of the east, to the wild and lonely coastline of the north. Oslo, Trondheim, Kristiansand, Stavanger, and Lillehammer make excellent tourist centres, apart from my favourite town of Bergen, and nearby Voss. Here are a few places of interest which can be easily reached in a day excursion, although it is advisable to leave by an early train to allow time to return and see more of one's destination and relax on the journey.

DAY TRIPS AND TIMES IN HOURS
Trondheim to Roros 3 hrs. Dombas 3 hrs. Namsos 4 hrs. Storlien 3 hrs.

Roros is an ancient mining town, with a healthy cold, dry climate, Dombas is a scenic mountain resort. Namsos is a small but thriving fishing port, while Storlien is a winter sports centre on the Swedish border.

Oslo to Halden 2½ hrs. Karlstad 3 hrs. Hamar 2 hrs. Lillehammer 3 hrs. Geilo 4 hrs.

Halden is situated near the Swedish border, and the old fortress with its magnificent view is well worth a visit. Karlstad, the capital of Varmland, is on Lake Vanern, the largest lake in Sweden. The town has fine buildings, wide streets, museums, spacious parks, and there is a local saying—"The sun is always shining in Karlstad."

Hamar has a highly·interesting railway museum, and one can take a boat trip from here on Lake Mjosa, Norway's largest lake, and there are some excellent shops in this manufacturing town.

Lillehammer is a thriving winter resort, on the wooded slopes to the east of Lake Mjosa, it has the famous Sandvig museum at Maihaugen, with a truly remarkable collection of Norwegian houses, an old Stave church, and farming implements.

Geilo is a busy mountain resort, both in Summer and Winter. Although rather small, it is very popular with the citizens of Oslo and Bergen, as well as the British, German and other nationalities.

Bergen to Voss 1½ hrs. Ulvik 2½ hrs. Stalheim 2½ hrs.

Famous for its luxury hotel set amongst magnificent scenery. Flam 4 hrs. Finse 3 hrs. Geilo 4 hrs. Balestrand 4 hrs.

Voss is an excellent centre for exploring the Hardanger and Sogne fjord areas.

Ulvik is ideally situated on the sheltered northern edge of the Hardanger fjord.

Flam is a small friendly village on the Aurland fjord, which has changed little with time. This delightful fjord village has two hotels, the Fretheim and Heimly, and in addition the guest houses Svingen and Solheim, and a camping site. Here is indeed "Heaven on Earth", away from the stress and strain of modern life and rush of the big cities. Flam is a "must" for all tourists who love and appreciate the peace and tranquil splendour of Norwegian nature.

And the Flam railway is truly unique, in a mere 12 miles (20 kilometres) one descends almost 3,000 feet, from the high mountain station of Myrdal, on the main Oslo-Bergen Railway, to the warm, sheltered Flam village, at the head of the Aurland fjord. The calm waters, sometimes blue, sometimes a little grey, reflect the awe-inspiring majesty of the surrounding high mountains. The Aurland fjord is an arm of the Sogne fjord, which is 110 miles long (180 kilometres) and is both the longest and deepest in Norway. The train even stops at Kjosfossen, a waterfall with a free fall of 292 ft., so that here, as elsewhere at small stations on this scenic route, one has the opportunity of taking photographs.

Finse is the highest station, 4,100 on the Bergen Railway, and is also the highest station in Northern Europe. It was near here, on the Hardanger glacier, where Scott of the Antarctic did much of his extensive training.

The whole journey from Bergen to Geilo is one of great contrasts and changes, for one climbs from sheltered fjords to steeply sloping hills and mountain pastures, pine and birch forests, and finally almost barren mountains, where even grasses and mosses find it hard to survive.

THE FLAM RAILWAY

The Scenic Railway to Happiness

Each year countless thousands of tourists from all corners of the world come to enjoy a remarkable journey on the Flam Railway, and return to their native land with happy and delightful memories.

This line is truly unique, owing to its steep gradient and great variety of scenery and climatic conditions, and in almost each single minute yet another vista is revealed to the attentive eye.

Leaving the main Oslo–Bergen Railway at Myrdal station, at an altitude of 2,860 ft. (880 metres) one notices the Alpine nature of the landscape, with snow still remaining on the mountain peaks, even at the height of summer, with dwarf birch trees, bog cotton, whortleberries, dwarf willows, mosses and hardy grasses struggling hard for survival. For nearly the first mile the track runs parallel to the main Bergen Railway, through sturdy snow tunnels, before making its first halt at Vatnahalsen, with its fine hotel and a superb view over the steep slopes of the Flam valley and surrounding high mountains. Another stop is made at the spectacular Kjosfossen waterfalls, and here one has a chance to use one's camera before seeing another view. Here the train slowly descends along an embankment to Bakli, and here can be seen the track higher up with the nearby mountain track which was also used in the construction of the Bergen Railway for transport of building materials. After passing through a long tunnel, one has a brief glimpse of the highest farm in the Flam valley, where about 3,000 goats are kept to make that delicious Norwegian goat cheese. The train continues on its steep descent and it is remarkable that there are no bridges on this track, in places the river has been made to alter course slightly by blasting holes through the mountain rocks below the track. There are 20 tunnels on this line which is 20 kilometres (12 miles) long and took 20 years to build.

At Berekvam station, which is exactly half-way down is a farming settlement with a few scattered farmsteads with their typical barns, known as stabbur, for storing hay as winter forage. Here the single track has given away to a short stretch of double track, the only place to do so on this remote mountain branch line. Wild flowers such as saxifrages, Alpine chickweed, eyebright, and pink valerian bloom in profusion. Further down this beautiful, winding valley one finds scabious, marjoram, meadow sweet, wild strawberries and raspberries.

Just past Dalsbotn is the mighty waterfall, Roandefossen, and if one has time the 5 mile walk from Dalsbotn to Flam is something not to be missed. Just before Hareina the valley widens out and the village of Flam can be seen below, with the picturesque Flam church, over 300 years old, and its mellow brown wooden structure blends so well with the surroundings. The vegetation of the lower Flam valley is very luxuriant, with smiling orchards of apple, pear, cherry, and plum trees, and well-kept gardens of vegetables, and bright flowers, sunflowers,

109

potentilla, rosa rugosa, a highly scented and hardy rose, marigolds, lobelia. In the springtime the meadows are covered with masses of dandelions and fruit trees and flowering shrubs in blossom.

Goats roam higher up amongst the rocks and gullies, and seals can often be observed in the nearby Naeroy fjord. The lovely light brown "Fjord horse" is a sturdy domesticated animal still used on the smaller and more remote farms. Other wild animals are the fox, stoat, mink, otter and marten. I have often seen a friendly red squirrel or wagtail near the Flam station or amongst the wooded grounds of the nearby Fretheim hotel. Sometimes the stately golden eagle slowly circles high above the fjord, and flocks of reindeer roam the mountain plateau.

From Flam one can take a frequent bus to the nearby village of Aurland, make a boat trip across the calm waters of the Sogne fjord to the beautiful resort of Balestrand with the renown Kvikne's Hotel. Boats make the long, scenic trip to Bergen, or to the village of Gudvangen on the Naeroy fjord, and proceed by bus to Stalheim and Voss.

One can take long walks in the mountains or just sit and watch the splendour of sea and sky, green valleys and rugged mountains and realise that here is a timeless, quiet, and unspoilt "HEAVEN ON EARTH", a heaven called "FLAM".

FROM DIARY OF A.W. SEARLEY 1899

Bergen July 17th. Visited the Hanseatic Museum and other places of interest. At 5 o'clock left by train for Voss. Rode on rear platform with our legs dangling over the line. 3 nice American girls joined us and we had a good time. Each time the train stopped all got out and photographed. Scenery very beautiful, but as there are 49 tunnels, many of which are very long, we all got black as sweeps. Slept at Fleischers at Voss. Very comfortable.

July 18th. Were called at 5.30. Got out at once and climbed up on high ground behind the village and "took" the church and snow-covered mountains. Drove to Stalheim in Stolkjaerre. Pony very strong and willing but a mouth like iron that made my hands sore; reins of rope. Scenery all the way here the unrolling of a panorama. Warm sunshine, no dust, good roads, easy gradient always upwards. Through pinewoods, past lakes and fosses, skirting round snow-covered mountains and passing fine salmon rivers. At Opheim saw about 50 large trout the result of a morning's fishing. Reached Stalheim about 1, had lunch and enjoyed good music. Small bottles of beer cost 1 kr. Walked down the slope and drove to Gudvangen. Many waterfalls, scenery majestically impressive S.S. "Ophir" could not come up Naeroy Fjord so went down about 8 miles in Norwegian steamer.

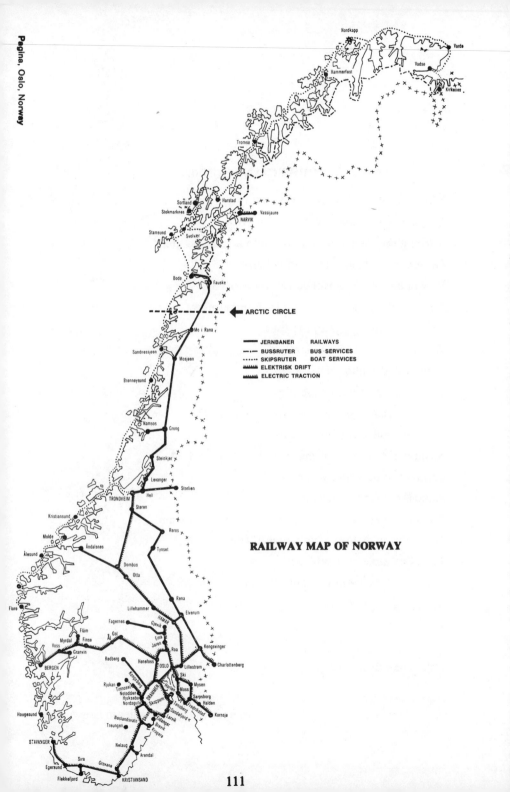

ARCTIC CIRCLE

JERNBANER	RAILWAYS
BUSSRUTER	BUS SERVICES
SKIPSRUTER	BOAT SERVICES
ELEKTRISK DRIFT	
ELECTRIC TRACTION	

RAILWAY MAP OF NORWAY

111

NORWEGIAN SUNSET

Clouds sweep swiftly across the Northern sky
The sun sets glowing in the purple West
Turning the clear heaven above into a splendid glory
Of light and shade and vivid colours
So wonderful—Too wonderful to describe
Yet full of untold beauty and infinite harmony
Changing, changing, all the time
And a million, million stars
A thousand million miles apart
Come out from darkening blue
Twinkling and sparkling—strong and bright
In a vast and silent World unknown
Spanning a universe of magic and mystery untold
Seeming so near and yet so far
Almost too far to imagine
As Night, like some long-awaited spellbound dream
Softly descends over Oslo's rugged fjiord
Ends like a blessing sublime
A joyous Day spent in a land so fair

Oslo—one September day.

THE NATIONAL ANTHEM OF FINLAND

Our land, our land, our fatherland, Sound loud, O name of worth!
No mount that meets the heaven's band.
No hidden vale, no wavewashed strand,
Is loved, as is our native North. Our own forefathers' earth.

Thy blossom, in the bud laid low, Yet ripened shall upspring.
See! From our love once more shall grow
Thy light, thy joy, thy hope, thy glow!
And clearer yet one day shall ring The song our land shall sing.

VARMLAND — SWEDEN

Clouds float like ships across the skies so blue
Birches green sway gently in the breeze
Here are woods and valleys
Far from the city's noise and hue
Where one finds peace and joy
And friends so kind and true.!!

A QUIET AND SINCERE DEDICATION

After many years of friendships, travel, and happy experiences, I dedicate
this book to the Scandinavian peoples and the youth of today.
The new generation now lives in the frightful chaos of the aftermath of
two World Wars.

May we steadfastly keep alive our love and Faith in Humanity, and our
Hope for the Future.!!

113

THE RAILWAYS OF SCANDINAVIA

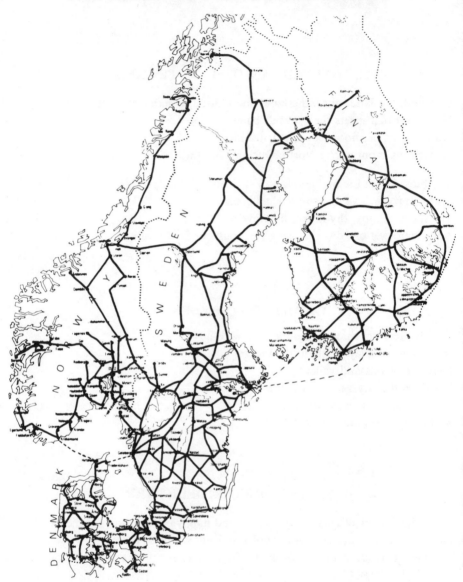

The State Railways of Denmark, Finland, Norway and Sweden are included on the Eurail Pass, and on Interail Cards.

There is also available the reasonably priced Nordturist Ticket (Scanrail Ticket) which may be purchased in Scandinavia as well as in the U.K,

All these give unlimited travel in Scandinavia.

APPENDIX

UPDATES: For Oslo Ostbahn read Oslo Sentral. From Summer 1989 all Bergen-Oslo trains will travel via Drammen, giving easy access to the Sorlandsbanen. On the Bergen-Drammen-Oslo route the longest tunnel is the six-mile Lier near Drammen. Next longest is Trollkona (opened 1988), east of Dale, and almost as long is the five-mile Ulriken tunnel that pierces the base of the mountain of that name to speed trains from Bergen to Arna.

ERRATA: Page 66: Read "Elva denotes bridges" as "Elva denotes river"; read Vosso for Stranda. Page 69: Read Reimegrad as Reimegrend. Page 85: Read Trornso as Tromso.

NORWAY

SORLANDSBANEN: This main line skirts the south coast of Norway but affords few sea views as along most of the route it runs inland. It gives a fine view of Mount Gausta, and the farmland of Jaeren is an interesting contrast to farms farther north. Sorlandsbanen serves Drammen, Kongsberg, Bo in Telemark, Arendal, Kristiansand (at the southern end of Setesdal), Flekkefjord and Stavanger, its western terminus.

KRODERBANEN: The Kroderbanen is a historic line and it is good that Norsk Jernbaneklubb has reopened it for steam trains on summer Sundays. Travelling in the well-preserved rolling stock we savoured the nostalgic hiss of steam on our ride from Vikersund (on the Drammen-Honefoss main line) to Kroderen on the south east tip of Lake Kroderen. On arrival at Kroderen we sampled the delicious waffles and pancakes freshly baked by club members.

HALLINGDAL: The Oslo-Bergen Railway runs through the Hallingdal. There is a once daily bus from Gol bus station (not the railway station) to Torpo, Hol and Aurland. A few daily buses also travel from Geilo to Hol, Aurland and Flam.

HEMSEDAL: Buses connect with Oslo-Bergen trains at Gol Railway Station for Hemsedal, Borgund, Laerdal, Revnes, Kaupanger and Sogndal.

NUMEDAL: Twice daily a bus travels through the Numedal from Geilo Railway Station to Dagali and Uvdal.

SWEDEN

The FRYKSDALEN Railway has been called Sweden's loveliest line. From Kil the little train wends its way north to Rottneros, Sunne (for Marbacka – Selma Lagerlöf's home – and the Kinship Memorial), and along Lake Fryken to Torsby, its terminus.

INLANDSBANEN: Swedish Railways have special offers for this line which links Gallivare, Ostersund, Orsa, Mora, Filipstad and Kristinehamn. Some sections must be covered by bus but, if energetic enough, one can pedal along parts of the track on a rail tricycle.

GOTHENBURG TO STROMSTAD: The line passes through Ytterby (with buses* to Kungalv and west to Marstrand), Uddevalla & Tanum (ancient rock drawings) to Stromstad, a busy summer seaside resort. Along the way are fine sea and pastoral views. (*Buses do not call at the station but the stationmaster will point out the bus stop along the road.) The ride to Marstrand includes two ferry crossings and provides some glorious coastal vistas. Marstrand, a tiny town on one of Bohuslan's many coastal islands, was idyllic on a warm September afternoon.

HALSINGBORG TO LUND: On another sunny September day we enjoyed the waterfront walk from Halsingborg main station to the northern terminus of the line to Lund and Malmo. Lund with its university and ancient cathedral was a delight. Next time we will spend longer in Lund and time our visit to go and view the great bird migration through Falsterbo, a short bus ride from Malmo.

FINLAND

In the Finnish State Railways Museum at Hyvinkää, between Helsinki and Tampere, we admire "Passi" built by Beyer, Peacock & Co., Manchester, England in 1868. Behind is "Latta Hattu" built in Finland in 1955. (Nearby is the only surviving one of the last Czar of Russia's sixteen Royal Trains).

INDEX OF PLACES NAMES

NORWAY
(Å or Aa is a sound at the end of the Norwegian alphabet.)

SWEDEN

COLOUR PLATES

* Vatnahalsen, Flåm Railway, Norway
* Kjosfossen, Flåm Railway, Norway
  Bergensbanen over Hardangervidda, Norway
* Dovresprinten at Otta, Norway
  Train near Flen, Sweden
* Narvik-Lulea Express at Abisko, Sweden
* Trains at Seinajoki, Finland
  Express crossing bridge, Finland

BLACK AND WHITE PHOTOGRAPHS

MAPS

(Cover and *photographs by Rosemary Plant)